COMPOSURE

COMPOSURE

HOW CENTERED LEADERS MAKE THE BIGGEST IMPACT

Zoë Routh

First published by Inner Compass Australia in August 2015

ISBN 978-0-9944119-0-7
Subjects: Success, Fulfilment, Leadership, Mindset, Motivation, Productivity

Author photograph by Hilary Wardaugh – hwp.com.au
Edited by Rebecca Stewart – thegallopingskirt.com
Typesetting, book design and printing by bookbound.com.au

For more information about the author
Zoë Routh
Email: zoe@innercompass.com.au
inner**compass**.com.au

Disclaimer
This book is intended to give general information only. The material herein does not represent professional advice. The author expressly disclaims all liability to any person arising directly or indirectly from the use of, or for any errors or omissions, the information in this book. The adoption and application of the information in this book is at the reader's discretion and is his or her sole responsibility.

CONTENTS

For truth tellers,
and the courage to dare the dragon

vii

Daring the dragon

*Sometimes in life we find ourselves face-to-face
with a dragon. It's not the one we expected,
and it's bigger than we imagined.*

Like you, I've had to face the dragon several times: when I was told I had cancer; at my father's bedside while he was on life support; in a firestorm of undermining by a once-trusted peer. It's in these moments we are confronted with the single most important decision of our lives: fight or flee.

What if there was another choice? What if we could confront the dragon, breathe in its fiery breath, look deep into its steely eyes and feel its coiled aggression writhing beneath the surface of its skin? In these moments we touch the dragon's heart and find, amazingly, it's our own.

The dragon is also an echo of our own deep pathologies, fears, and small ego tremors. Cancer is the manifestation of stress. A work enemy the mirror of jealousy. The dying parent a reminder of all one's own failings and regrets. It's in the deep crucible of black despair and fear that we discover compassion. For others first, and finally, for ourselves.

Being fully present to the dragon, in all its wild and dangerous fury, we suddenly know we can dare the dragon to serve, not slay.

There is, in our darkest moments, a light. In the depths of fog, a small clearing. We discover we are not only tethered to the universe, we are the universe. We are its face, its hands, and its heart. Our duality dissolves and in its stead, unity.

Daring the dragon requires deep composure. The kind of composure anchored not through conscious thought, but through conscious living. Conscious living is the discipline and practice of self-inquiry, a curious mind, an open heart. It is how we align our actions with values in a purpose of service. Conscious living keeps us anchored to a deep and abiding sense of the present moment, while being aware and beholden to history, posterity, and the higher realms of spirit. It allows us to inhabit a world built on and imagined by duality, while being guided by a sense of oneness, of connection, of expansion.

Conscious living is the hallmark of centered leaders.

These are the leaders who find themselves in the midst of crisis, and the unknown, who remain unflustered, even stoic. While others feel the heat rising, hearts beating hammer and tongs, ready for bloody battle. Centered leaders can cut through histrionics and heated conversation with a gesture, a word, a smile. Their mere presence reassures, and cloaks others in a blanket of quiet confidence. They can quiet rattling sabres and bring parties back to the negotiation table.

Centered leaders have an aura about them. It's not their message, nor their brilliance. It's how they move. It's how they smile. Everything is just clean and decisive. Who they are on the inside radiates outwards in a congruent message. They resonate with authenticity.

In the presence of a centered leader, we feel embraced and honoured as a unique and precious being.

Our world needs centered leaders more than ever. Technology has fast-tracked our connectivity, so ideas and their emotions spread like grassfire across the globe. If we are to survive extremism, we need leaders at every level steeped in composure: broadcasting love, not hate.

In our own lives, the ability to operate with grace under fire becomes an imperative rather than a nice-to-have. Our bodies are not built for the continuous bombardment of information and stimuli; our brains are overloaded with terabytes of input in every given moment. Our nervous system is under chronic assault, keeping us perpetually primed for a fight to the death. Despite all of this we are expected to perform and contribute in a professional, even-keeled manner, especially when the stakes are high.

The capacity to remain centered has become a personal survival requirement as well as a professional asset.

Then there are moments, possibly in a crisis, when we realise that we might be the calmest person in the room. We realise we are going to have step up, and be the leader, even if we don't have authority or positional influence. We need to rely on our inner clarity and conviction to do what is right, and what is needed.

On December 15th 2014, Man Haron Monis entered the Lindt Café in Sydney Australia. He pulled a gun and locked the doors, holding 18 people hostage. After a 16-hour standoff, a gunshot was heard and the police stormed the café. Hostage Tori Johnson was killed by Monis. Another hostage, Katrina Dawson, was killed by a police bullet ricochet in the subsequent raid. Monis was also slain.

I sometimes wonder if I had been one of the unfortunate people trapped in the café. If, on a tightrope between life and death, whether I'd have had the composure required to find a space in my heart for love, and not fear at the end of a gun. I can never know, nor do I wish for a situation to test my resolve.

I do know however that whether it be a life and death crisis, a professional challenge, or a personal test, centered leadership practice helps send down a sturdy keel to hold the boat steady through the tempest. This steady composure helps others to navigate the storm as well.

Here on these pages it is my intention to reveal the map to composure and centered leadership. The world needs more cool heads and steady hands at the helm; I invite yours to be there too.

Zoë Routh, Canberra 2015

'Centered' or 'centred'? There was no definitive agreement on which spelling to choose. After consultation it was decided that the spelling of this word was slowly leaning more and more towards the American version, 'centered'. As a British-born, Canadian-raised, and Australian-naturalised person, I had no particular preference either way. So we've adopted the spelling that seems easier on the eye and following social trend: 'centered'.

Citations and texts I mention are listed in the appendices by chapter.

Zoë Routh

Introduction

Our world is shifting. It is fraught with perils, caverns, and hidden bogs. Dragons – both internal and external – lurk, ready to catch us unaware. In this changeable world, linear approaches will not do. We need flexibility and change agility. We need leaders who can operate with cool heads and warm hearts, regardless of external circumstances. We operate best through the development of our leadership thinking, doing, being, and presence.

The dragon's kingdom

Our world, the dragon's kingdom, is furious and frenzied. Technology has created transparency and connectedness across cultures and borders. Today all we need to set up a business is a mobile phone and an internet connection. Financial empowerment is escalating dramatically at a micro level while at the macro level, global financial entanglement is thicker and thornier than ever.

Interconnected economies

World economies are now woven together in ways more volatile than before the British Empire. The Global Financial Crisis of 2007 brought the world to its knees in a hacking cough. China's demand for minerals has created a burgeoning Western Australian economic belt, only to see that belt tightened drastically as demand has fallen away. Fortunes were made and careers accelerated, only to be dropped a few short years later. Our interconnected economies represent chaos theory magnified.

Global transparency

Social media has given us reading glasses on the world, and Google Maps a global microscope. In this era of transparency, renegade leaders cannot escape scrutiny. From 2011-2014 the world watched as Egyptians steered their country through a revolution to place Mohamed Morsi at the helm. His dictatorial intentions became apparent: he granted himself unlimited powers to 'protect' the nation, and the power to legislate without judicial oversight. A second revolution followed, with Abdel Fattah al-Sisi elected in somewhat dubious processes. Stability has nonetheless followed.

All the events were reported in a tangible and personal way though social media. This public narrative created pressure never seen before in political spheres. Social media's power for social and political change has been revealed, and privacy is gone. Transparency – and hopefully accountability – are the new norm.

Entertainment distribution

Disruption and volatility extend beyond political and social spheres to significant communication channels. Curation, and not monopoly of distribution, is the new entertainment modality. Spotify has upended the music industry model. Entertainment streamed online has sounded the death knell of TV and radio. Specialisation, exclusion, and niche markets are the new mode of entertainment. Gone are the days of appealing to mass media.

Consumer flexibility

Retail shopping in its current form is dying. Trudging to the mall to browse is seen as a waste of time rather than a pastime. The rise of online shopping has liberated consumers from local restrictions and territorial limits and the retail sector is struggling to keep up with changes in consumer behaviour. Store after store closes their doors as they fail to reinvent a service that suits contemporary and emerging trends.

Global trends and leadership

In this volatile landscape, what kind of leadership do we need? Certainly black-and-white thinking falls short of addressing the complexity and interconnectedness of our world. The ability to access all aspects of our cognitive and emotional abilities, however, will give us a chance to stay the course regardless of the storm. This is the evolution of our leadership thinking, doing, being, and presence.

1. Leadership thinking

In the pivotal leadership text *Spiral Dynamics*, Don Beck and Christopher Gowan outline the communal consciousness (what they call 'cultural memes') of various global cultures. Each consciousness evolves out of its particular context, a particular set of circumstances.

Around the world, cultures span from tribal concerns through to global orientation. In the latter there is a growing concern for global interconnectedness, environmental care and custodianship for the entire planet and all sentient beings. Largely we find that where cultures are concerned with meeting basic human needs, the focus is on tribal, if not individual survival. War-torn areas like Somalia are an example.

Some nations are evolving into a more global orientation. European nations are experiencing this evolution first-hand as they realise the inter-dependency of their economic links with the Euro. Helping one another, such as ensuring the financial viability of Greece, ensures the prosperity of all. We also see high-profile leaders spearheading global custodianship. Sir Richard Branson's group the Elders raises awareness and campaigns to redress international wrongs as a global responsibility. Their concerns include educating women and girls as a pivot point for improving standards of living, ending the conflict in the Middle East, and addressing climate change.

In *Spiral Dynamics*, Beck and Cowan contend that our leaders need to learn the patterns of memes within cultures and the patterns of conflicts. They assert that this will not only help leaders to bridge possible differences, but also help humanity evolve into a more peaceful, abundant state.

Profound leadership thinking acknowledges that the more intricately connected we become, the more we need to change as leaders.

George W. Bush asserted in his post-9/11 address to Congress: "Either you are with us, or you are with the terrorists." Such black-and-white thinking is now being denigrated across all popular culture.

In *Star Wars Episode 3: Revenge of the Sith* (2005), hero-turned-villain Anakin Skywalker decrees to his long-time mentor and father figure, "If you're not with me, then you're my enemy." Obi-Wan relies, "Only a Sith deals in absolutes."

There is a chilling echo of Sith Lord-like absolutes in every global conflict. Muslim versus Christian. Sunni versus Shiite. Palestinian versus Israeli. Democratic versus Imperial.

In the deep dive into our humanity, we discover there is no 'axis of evil'[1]. There are simply multiple perspectives. We find that we are in this world together, despite our differences.

2. Leadership doing

The five-year business plan must be energised. Organisations need change agility, to be proactive and nimble. The adage 'innovate or die' has never been more true. We need to steer our boat through turbulence or risk being swamped and taken under.

Leadership action needs to be quick, decisive, and focused. It also needs to be developed with a greater global context in mind, and the consideration of historical influence and impact on future generations.

The context for leadership action is no longer local, contained, and immediate. It is global, interconnected, and long term.

3. Leadership being

We need leaders who can stand in their own truth, navigate the truths of others, and bridge the divide and co-create a reality that

---

1   US President George W. Bush used the phrase 'Axis of Evil' in his State of the Union Address on January 29, 2002, and repeated it often throughout his presidency to describe governments he accused of helping terrorism and seeking weapons of mass destruction. From Wikipedia: https://en.wikipedia.org/wiki/Axis_of_evil

supports all. This requires an enormous amount of self-awareness and inner calm.

As Cindy Wigglesworth says in *SQ 21: The 21 Skills of Spiritual Intelligence*, self-awareness requires 'spiritual intelligence': the ability to make wise and compassionate decisions while maintaining inner and outer equanimity, regardless of circumstances. Spiritual intelligence harnesses the best of the mind (the rational) with the best of the heart (the emotional) to make more considered, and positive influential decisions.

We need leaders who can lead with the best of the head (wisdom) and the best of the heart (compassion). Spirit talks through a third dimension: the instinct and the inner voice of the Higher Self. This what we feel in our gut.

We need leaders who are full-bodied: leaders who lead with head, heart, and gut.

4. Leadership presence

Our leadership presence amplifies influence. If our leadership thinking, doing, and being are aligned, then we need to be sure the projection of ourselves is highly tuned and resonant. How we show up has an impact on how we're heard, if we're heard. Not only are we the package of our ideas, we are the embodied representation of possibility and confidence.

We become a flame, a lighthouse for others. We are part of the system that supports a new idea whose time has come. We give courage, sustain hope, and inspire action.

Our inner world of head, heart, and soul moves into the world when we decide it's time to broadcast and connect. For our message to be heard, it needs to chime as clearly as a fine crystal glass. We need deep, sonorous composure.

Let's do that.

LEADER FOCUS: Dr. Kiran Bedi

India's highest ranking female police officer, UN representative, tennis champion, and former Inspector General of one of the world's largest prisons.

"Are you leading your life or living your life?"

Dr Kiran Bedi stared with a piercing gaze at each of the participants. They shifted awkwardly in their seats.

One of them squeaked, "Leading…?"

"That's right. You need to be *leading* your life. If you are simply living your life, you are not a leader. If you are to be a leader, you need to be uncomfortable, you need to grow, and you need to give. That is the way I lead my life: give, grow, go."

In 2014 I was on a two-week study tour of India with the Australian Rural Leadership Program (ARLP) as group facilitator. Seeing Dr Bedi for the first time made me weep like a star-struck teenager.

Dr Bedi is someone who rocks boats. She experienced a lot of resistance to her criticism of corrupt politicians and issues in the police force, and in an attempt to silence her, she was sent to Tihar Prison in 1993 to be Inspector General. They expected her to fail dramatically. With over 11,000 inmates – men, women, adolescents, children, Indians and foreigners – this was one of the largest prisons in the world. It was rife with corruption, abuse, and drugs. Fear and bullying were endemic, bribery *de rigueur*.

Dr Bedi documents her experiences and approach in I*t's Always Possible: Transforming One Of The Largest Prisons In The World.* Instead of failing as expected, she transformed the prison into an ashram, a place of learning where she introduced Vipassana meditation. As Inspector General, Dr Bedi allowed, for the first time, non-government organisations in for humanitarian projects such as education of children, health services and more. When she was transferred from prison as an inmate a few years later (the effort to humiliate her having failed spectacularly), the prisoners rioted in protest at her removal.

How does a leader wield such influence?

Clearly Dr Bedi's reputation and achievements create a sense of gravitas and awe about her. Before she was a national hero, she was one woman swimming against the tide. What is it about her that invites respect, awe, and surrender? I found a window into her influence while listening to her speak with the ARLP participants over lunch.

One asked: "Where do you get your energy from? You clearly have many responsibilities and plenty of political pressure. What sustains you?"

Dr Bedi replied: "It is my connection to Source. Every day, I close my eyes and connect with the infinite. Every day is an opportunity to give. Every day is an opportunity to learn. If I make a mistake, it's OK as long as I learn, and apply what I learn. If I don't know what to do, I pray. That is what happened in Tihar. On my third day there, I walked around the prison and entered one of the largest wards, all men. And they came over to see me, apprehensive and curious about the new Inspector General, a woman no less! So what did I do?

"I said to them, 'do you pray?' They did not answer and looked at each other, surprised. 'I said, do you pray?' Someone answered, 'yes ma'am', and I said, 'Good. Let us pray.' So I picked a popular song they would know and I led them in singing a prayer together."

In the face of such complex and seeming insurmountable issues, Dr Bedi reached out to the tenuous thread of their common humanity. Whatever had led them to prison, they were in this together, as fellow human beings, and she would make every decision from that premise.

Her desire to make life better for her fellow human beings dropped a deep anchor of conviction and focus that allowed her to buffet the resistance and obstacles that arose with each new initiative.

Connection and commitment: these are Dr. Kiran Bedi's inner compass points.

The secret to composure: from roadblocks to broadcast channels

The world needs centered leaders with a powerful voice. Like Dr Kiran Bedi, we may have a strong commitment to making a difference and leading a purposeful life. We are competent, intelligent, and insightful. But are people listening? Do we get a say? How can we be more effective at commanding attention without shouting?

As leaders, there are three major obstacles to being heard:

Roadblock 1: The 'other people' problem

Many leaders are frustrated that they are not given fair opportunities or consideration by others, a feeling that includes peers, supervisors, and other stakeholders. The challenge is in projecting a centered presence that represents our talents in a way that drowns out any subconscious (or conscious) cognitive bias due to our race, gender, size, or other differentiating factors.

Roadblock 2: Roared whispers

Sometimes it's not what we say, it's how we say it. Sometimes, it's both. Our engagement style, expressed through our stress filters, affects how our voice and message is received by others. How do we get cut through and be heard when we may be hampered by lack of authority, visibility, or presentation effectiveness?

Roadblock 3: Leader-in-training

The biggest hurdle is often an internal one. Our own self-doubts combined by lack of leadership prowess can scramble our message and project incompetence, timidity, and lack of decisiveness.

The good news is that with a few key strategies, insightful frameworks, and a strong service mindset, we can overcome our own roadblocks and become the leaders we want to follow. As Ralph Waldo Emerson said: "Who you are speaks so loudly I can't hear what you're saying."

Cindy Wigglesworth describes a leader as "a calm and healing presence, one who can respond with wisdom and compassion regardless of circumstances, with inner and outer equanimity."[2] A calm and healing presence may seem unachievable if we're being bumped from one screaming priority to another. However, with cultivated awareness and practice, this can indeed become the embodied centered presence we aspire to adopt and project.

If we are compelling and attractive, people want to watch, listen, and pay attention.

If we show up stressed, unfocused, and reactive, it's like we're broadcasting our message via a handheld camcorder from the '80s: shaky, fuzzy, and garbled. Developing a centered leadership presence demands clear connection, HD, surround sound, and Retina Display! Evolving over several levels a leader can start at a point of pure survival and emerge into an intuitive leader, with the insight and courage to lead others.

At the heart of evolution is how we manage stress. This is based on deep self-awareness and self-mastery. As a result, there are different levels of how we engage with others. As we evolve as centered leaders, reduce our stress, increase our presence, and evolve our capacity for influence.

The Composure and Connection Ladder

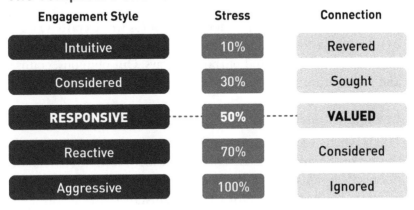

Engagement Style	Stress	Connection
Intuitive	10%	Revered
Considered	30%	Sought
RESPONSIVE	50%	VALUED
Reactive	70%	Considered
Aggressive	100%	Ignored

---

2 https://www.deepchange.com/uploads/resource_article/file_name/3/ SpiritualIntelligenceEmotionalIntelligence2011.pdf, p.4

Level 1: Aggressive

This is survival mode. When we are 100 per cent stressed it is because we are simply focused on meeting our core needs, or are under threat. At this level we are going to project aggression, antagonism, and prickliness. Our message is lost in the roar of our chaos.

Level 2: Reactive

Otherwise a calm and considered person, we may jump when our buttons get pressed. It seems we are often on the defensive. It's one step up from survival, but not far! We may not appear as a raging tiger, perhaps more of a screeching hyena. People pay attention and consider our message, but more from wariness than respectful embrace.

Level 3: Responsive

This is a turning point. We have enough self-mastery and self-awareness to breathe, and pause before sharing our view. We come across as thoughtful, reflective, patient, and focused. As a result, our colleagues respect our opinion and our contributions are valued.

Level 4: Considered

The depth and richness of our thinking, the quality of our interactions, and the deep inner peacefulness we've crafted allows us to present a considered, rich message. The clarity of our thoughts reaches others in deep and purposeful ways. Our opinions, counsel, and presence are sought.

Level 5: Intuitive

This is where leaders become fully present and aware, the calm in the eye of the storm. We are able to consider multiple stakeholder perspectives, long-term consequences and various pathways, then generate the best option for that circumstance. In our presence, others simply relax and feel better around us. We are both revered and loved, for own sake as well as for the vision, courage, and insight we bring to our tribe.

So how do we move from reactive to intuitive? How do we become centered? How do we develop composure?

**Composure
is a dance between
human *doing* and human *being*,
flowing between a focus on
self and *others*.**

Balancing human doing and human being between the focus on self and others emerges into six key areas in this book.

Chapter 1: Growth
Framing the quest

We start by knowing our 'Big Why'. This is what gets up out of bed in the morning and calls us forward to make a contribution and a difference. We outline the key principles that will guide us through challenges. These focus around our leadership thinking, being, and doing. We'll also get clear on knowing what feeds the soul. This is our passion, value, and talents.

Chapter 2: Focus
Choosing the quest

We'll move from the 'why' of our quest to the how and what. We'll get clear on our plans that span our hundred years on the planet down to our daily plans. We'll get equipped for the journey by looking at our personal brand, or our 'coat of arms'. We'll choose archetypes that can help balance our leadership approach. Lastly we'll craft a map to guide us based on challenges we choose for our own personal and professional growth.

Chapter 3: Contribution
The crucible in the dragon's lair

This chapter is about understanding how we can live though the challenges that transform us, to make us stronger as a result. These pressures, fears, and challenges heat the cauldron of experience that serves as a crucible. Once we discover how to survive our own crucible experiences, we can help others do the same. Once we learn to help individuals to face their own dragons, we learn to prepare and take a team through crucible experiences together.

Chapter 4: Connection
Taming the dragon with grace under fire

This chapter is about 'emotional aikido'. This is the adventurer's chief battle weapon in managing our own emotions and those of others. This is where we learn to stay steady at the helm when everything else is turbulent and ferocious.

Chapter 5: Renewal
The road home, or the road out again

On every journey, we need to stop, take stock, and recharge. This is the time to assess what stays and what goes in our adventure. We follow the basic principle of the cycles of creation and destruction: clear out the old to make way for the new.

Chapter 6: Oneness
The path of totality

For centered leaders with deep composure, there is a balance of being and doing, of focus on self and others. This ebb and flow distils from a primary, overarching truth: a deep and abiding sense of oneness. Centered leaders have the ability to be fully present and immersed in the moment, while focused on future plans. In this chapter we will examine how to live in courage and faith, while being tethered to our sense of oneness.

I invite you now to explore the quest to become a centered leader. At the end may you weather any storm, and stay calm at the helm.

Framing The Quest

*Many authors have written about finding purpose,
and how to follow it faithfully. But what is it exactly?
And how do we find it, let alone follow it?
How do we articulate our quest into an actionable
framework for our life?*

Centered leaders feel a deep connection to a purpose greater than themselves. They live in a tension between meeting personal needs, and serving a higher calling. Both are important, but their personal needs are satisfied in service to the bigger cause.

So how do we choose or discover this higher cause?

Lance Secretan's simple approach, outlined in *The Spark, The Flame, and the Torch* suggests a way of discovering what he calls your "burning inner passion". He calls threats to this journey the "'Terra threats': the things that spoil the world for us – or that have the potential to threaten or wound the world and cause serious global damage if we don't change or reverse them." (pp.44-47)

If we extend this concept, we choose our purpose between horror and beauty.

When we look at the biggest problem in the world, the horror, and then look to the beauty in the world, our purpose is revealed.

What we see is the revelation of our calling; our purpose is to help bridge the gap between the two. Taking an antidote approach has the potential to create a black-and-white view of the world. I would build a polarity and look for balance and harmony in the opposites.

INSIGHT

Find compassion to balance hate

For me, the biggest horror in the world is war. It stems from a lack of compassion, from hatred and prejudice. The beauty I see in the world is love and peace. To bridge the two, I seek to promote greater understanding and compassion in the world. The quest for wisdom and compassion in my own life extends to how I work with clients and my mission to help create better leaders for a better world.

It's not about resisting hate and war, but healing it and balancing it with compassion. We can't hate if we feel compassion. Compassion trumps hate; it doesn't eliminate it.

Horrors are the heat that transforms fuel into fire. Each of us is an unkindled blaze of passion, values, and talent, until we know our 'why' and the fire is lit.

Simon Sinek speaks of the importance of knowing your why in his book *Start With Why*. He contends that great leaders speak from the 'why' first (the part of us linked to our limbic system, our emotional centre). This part of us resonates with great callings and universal truths that elevate our thinking and feelings to new levels of consciousness.

He calls this the Golden Circle of Communication. It starts with the inner circle of 'why', then to the next ring of 'how' and then third circle of 'what'.

In his 2009 TEDx[3] talk, Sinek uses the example of how Apple markets their technology. Apple communicates the why first:

---

3 How Great Leaders Inspire Action: http://www.ted.com/talks/simon_sinek_ how_great_leaders_inspire_action?language=en

"Everything we do is designed to challenge the status quo, of doing things differently." Then they go on to their 'how' and 'what': "The way we challenge the status quo is by producing beautiful designed, easy-to-use technology. We just happen to make great computers."

In marketing, many other organisations make these points in reverse: they explain what they do and how they do it, the 'how 'being their unique selling proposition or point of difference. Many do not speak to their big 'why'.

An example of what Apple might have said if they communicated like any other technology company: "We make beautifully designed easy-to-use computers. (How) They've got great user-friendly features (What). Want to buy one?" As Sinek says: 'meh'.

Sinek repeats the refrain: "People don't buy what you do, they buy WHY you do it." So if we are to be centered leaders with influence and reach, we need to tune in to our 'why', then our 'how' and 'what'.

I've added here a slight variation to Simon's Golden Circle to map out our personal purpose:

1. We start with Why: Knowing that our purpose is to bridge and reconcile horror and beauty.

2. Then we move to How: We focus on our personal principles that guide our quest.

3. Then we move to What: This is what we will focus on that fuels our soul.

4. Finally we move to a quest: A quest is a smaller adventure in the greater scheme of our lives. A quest might last one year, or many years, or even just a few months. Having quests keeps us focused, fuelled, and growing.

First, reinvent the hero

We all grew up with stories of heroes. From the comic book characters of Superman, Spiderman, and Wonder Woman, through to fairy tales of the dashing prince saving the damsel in distress and religious icons like Jesus and Mohammad. The hero story pervades our collective psyche.

Joseph Campbell writes extensively about the hero story across human cultures. It's part of who we are, how we think about life and its challenges, and what it means to have a life of purpose. The hero has gotten a bad rap of late in leadership thinking.

The idea that there is one person (usually male) who can save the day, make things better, and bring hope to the world, is rife. US Presidential candidate races are run on this premise; it's all about the individual.

We idolise and make much of the person 'out in front': the army general, the CEO, the politician. Why is this now a problem?

Our cultural context is completely different.

We live in an interconnected world with complex challenges that go across borders and cultures that will affect many generations hence. If we think one person is going to fix it all then we are blind to the world of our own making, and equally held back in addressing the issues. Put simply, the world is too big and too complex for one mind alone.

We are in this together. We need collective, collaborative, and creative thinking to steer our planet safely through its threats.

There is a place for the reinvented hero in leadership, however, and it's deeply personal. To consider ourselves as heroes is not only inspiring, but incredibly useful. To see our lives as a series of quests, of challenges to overcome, of new abilities and insights gained, then to bring that wisdom back to the village for the greater good: this is a framework and a story that gives our lives meaning and purpose.

To see our lives as a hero's journey (thank you Joseph Campbell) keeps us mobilised and focused on evolution – of ourselves and our world. We lose the sense of "I'm too small to make a difference" and gain "I'm small, so I am the difference." Our journey becomes a thread in the tapestry, essential to the pattern, but not the pattern itself. We can celebrate the individual hero for their own unique contribution, rather than seeking the hero as having the contribution.

Each hero's journey is thus part of the story of the world's hero's journey: we are not trying to save the world, we are trying to save ourselves, and in doing so, the world is saved.

So, heroes – onwards! There are mountains to climb and dragons to tame.

Three principles to frame the quest

Principles are the pillars of our soul's home. They are the rules and framework for all our choices and how we engage in the world. They are like the knight's special weapons and code of chivalry; it is what helps keep them true to their quest.

As ethical, world-oriented leaders, we need to match personal principles with universal laws. Personal principles provide the ethical framework for all our choices. If we base them on universal principles in service to the world and our greater 'why', then we will emerge with our own moral commandments.

Centered leaders develop personal principles in three key aspects of leadership: Being, Thinking, and Doing. The objective is to create a filter to make choices that create a positive difference. Here are some examples:

Being

- Be present
- Choose confidence
- Avoid struggle
- Let go of anger
- Choose forgiveness
- Be peaceful
- Connect

Thinking

- Learn to accept responsibility for everything in one's life
- Choose faith over fear
- Seek opportunity
- Forgive past wrongs and learn from them
- Detach from expectations and outcomes
- Choose appreciation over worry
- Focus on purpose with unrelenting enthusiasm and persistence

Doing

- Serve with love and joy
- Be generous
- Offer massive value
- Under promise and over deliver
- Treat others with love, kindness, and respect
- Take massive action in alignment with purpose and goals
- Rest, recover, renew.

INSIGHT

Staying the course

It's not easy to live all of these principles every day. I have rough spots that chafe my daily activity, which are little reminders that I'm not always living the best version of myself.

There are times when my inner critic gets the best of me and I find myself wallowing in doubt and fear. I start to worry about my projects, wondering if they'll be successful, and then berate myself for poor results.

When I'm busy with self-criticism, I feel small and sensitive. I definitely don't feel centered, calm, and confident. When I'm in this shrunken state, I know I'm not focused on service to others and making a difference.

I use these guiding principles to serve as gentle reminders to come back to center. Whenever I'm feeling off-balance, I reconnect with the principles and stabilise once more.

A quest must feed the soul

Centered leaders choose lives that feed the soul at all levels. The soul bridges the connection of the ego self to the universal mind through the experience of joy, happiness, and fulfilment. This is achieved by matching what we cherish with what we love to do and what we are best at.

We feed the soul by ensuring our quest is based on three key things:

1. Values – what we cherish and hold dear
2. Passions – what we love to do
3. Talents – what we are good at

LEADER FOCUS: Bianca Jurd

Outdoor leader and adventurer goes on a quest to live waste-free for a year.

In 2014, Bianca Jurd left her job without knowing 'what' to do. She wanted a change and a new quest. Her 'Terra threat' centered on abuse of the environment. As an avid outdoor adventurist and outdoor leader, the beauty she saw was in the natural world.

In clarifying her quest, Bianca asked herself these key questions:

- What do I love to do and what gives me joy?
- What are my unique talents? What do I feel born to do?
- What matters the most to me?

She answered them this way:

- What do I love to do? I love to create. To draw. To build.
- What are my unique talents? Seeing the gifts and joy in small moments, in small things.
- What matters most to me? Living softly on the planet, connecting with others, improving the environment.

From these answers was born her great quest: to live waste-free for a year.

Bianca and her partner Nic set about researching strategies to reduce their household waste to zero. For a whole year.

Then she combined her passion (to create), talent (seeing gifts and joy in small things), and values (living softly on the planet, connecting with others, making a difference) to create a blog and share the project with the world. She wrote to uplift and inspire others to at least reduce, if not eliminate, their contribution to landfill.

Bianca and Nic tackled their home and found solutions to tricky problems. Bianca applied her creative and building talents to re-purposing the items she didn't know how to re-use or recycle. She rebuilt an old set of drawers to store waste while they looked for recycling or re-purposing solutions. Not happy with a big black box in their home, Bianca re-painted it in glorious colours with "Get me waste free" emblazoned across it.

She has also discovered another talent – quirky, frank, and authentic writing. Her blog is a joy to read.

You can read more about Bianca's quest at www.wastefreeme.com

Since reading Bianca's blog, I've changed my own behaviour. I am now diligent about recycling soft plastics (including cling wrap!), looking for no or low packaging options, and composting as much as possible.

When seeking the Why of our quest, like Bianca Jurd, we can achieve harmony when talent, values, and passions align in service to the greater Why of our quest.

Key Points for Growth

Identify your Big Why

- Reflect on the 'Terra threat' from your perspective. See if you can reduce it to one big pivotal challenge.
- Identify what would balance or bring harmony to this threat? This becomes your Big Why.

Fine tune your quest principles

Write down what your key guiding principles are in the leadership realms of Thinking, Being, and Doing.

Prepare for the quest by knowing what feeds the soul

Reflect and journal the following:

1. Values – what you cherish and hold dear
2. Passions – what you love to do
3. Talents – what you are good at.

CHAPTER 2: FOCUS

Choosing The Quest

*Now we move from our why to the how of our quest.
We dive deeply into the nitty-gritty of our theme
and what will frame our activity for the next week,
quarter, year, and decades ahead. Like any journey,
we will need to make preparations and become equipped. On
the hero's journey, that means focusing on what character
traits, qualities, and plans will best support us
as we venture forwards into the unknown.*

I see quests as a type of adventure. Adventure is one of my core values. It's taken me up mountains, down wild rivers, across hemispheres and cultures, and through the darkest rabbit holes of my own psyche.

I bring adventure to all aspects of my life and work. It's not always 'extreme' like running a marathon or going cross-country skiing (and I do a lot of that too), but it is intentional and deliberate. It's how I keep enjoying the ride, as well as ensuring there is a ride to be had!

The difference between adventure and misadventure, however, is the quality of the planning.

Prepare the plans

We start with the end in mind. We map our life plan in reverse. Start with the lifetime and legacy vision first. This is how we want work and life to contribute to the evolution of humanity and our planet. This is the big 'why'. Review the first chapter on Growth to flesh this out.

From here, we reverse engineer life in 20-year blocks (assuming a long-lived life of 100). Choose a theme word for each of those twenty years and how you want them to feel. For example, 40 to 60 might be 'learning' or 'progress'.

Once we come to our nearest current decade, start adding in detail. This is the 'how' and 'what' being made a bit clearer. Choose a big picture theme word for the current 10-year block. For example, the 40s might be about 'parenting' or 'nurture', the 50s might be about 'contribution', and the 60s might be about 'harvest'.

From there we boil it down to a one-year plan, complete with theme word, holidays and experiences, who we want to spend time with, what we want to learn, how we want to beautify our home.

Then we plan it out in 90-day projects mapped against quarters. These then break down into weekly plans, followed by daily plans.

Checklist of plans
- Lifetime and legacy vision; the Big Why
- 20-year blocks with feeling theme words
- Current decade theme word
- Current one-year plan: theme word, holidays, experiences, people to spend time with, what to learn, how to beautify the home
- 90-day projects
- Weekly plans
- Daily plans.

INSIGHT

Finding my quest theme for the year

Each year I choose a new 'quest' theme word to help frame the nature of my adventures. Last year's word was *joie de vivre* (the enjoyment of life). I wanted to savour all the moments of a busy and brilliant year. It helped to remind me of how to approach my day, my projects, and my reflection time. And I wanted a change from the 'hard', 'struggle', and 'tense' that is my Achilles heel in stress management. *Joie de vivre* helped remind me to say 'yes' to fun, and 'no' to bad attitudes and decisions.

I also like to make my theme quest word come alive. This year, *connection* is my theme word. For me this means reaching out, engaging with others with compassion and genuineness. It means growing my tribe focused on my purpose of 'better leaders, better world', and my passion of helping leaders love who they are and what they do in service to the world.

I then chose the image of a sunflower to represent my quest word. The connection part is found in all the exquisite perfection of the seeds. It reminds me that nature and the world is truly inspired and magical, with more detail and order than can be manufactured. It reminds me to trust the Universe, trust the connection between all things and a sense of Divine order. It represents beauty and growing tall, while being courageous to risk being a 'tall poppy'.

In creating and anchoring our quest theme word, we can make a shrine of it. A totem or piece of jewellery serves as reminder or talisman. A poster or an image is a good visual anchor, which can also become a new screensaver. Reminders on your phone can say: "I am deeply connected" and "connect deeply with others."

A quest theme gives us texture, focus, and flavour for the articulation of our purpose in the world. It also helps us galvanise into action. After all, a quest is just a wish without taking some action in pursuit of it.

Developing personal brand as a coat of arms

While presence is how we show up, brand is how others see us. Ideally, we want our brand to be in alignment with our purpose. We also want that to be readily perceived by others. We want our integrity and authenticity to radiate naturally.

Our brand is like a coat of arms. Medieval knights had a coat of arms to link them with a particular family or heritage. Ancient Roman militia used symbols on their shield as a way of identifying military units. We want our brand or coat of arms to be a unique expression of self, yet easily recognised by others. This is not to set ourselves above others, but to draw in people with like-minded values.

We can influence perception of brand when we channel our message intentionally through our chosen brand qualities. How do we craft our personal brand, our personal coat of arms? Imagine a trusted colleague being asked for a reference about you. What would you like them to say? Imagine them talking about your personality, talent, and capability. This is the start of your personal brand coat of arms.

Our job after this is to bring daily awareness to our behaviour, thinking, and engagement. We check that we are consistent in our desired brand and what we are actually projecting.

One way to stay anchored in our brand, our coat of arms, is to dress the part. Physical cues in our environment can trigger desired responses, and help us establish the best emotional state.

Some personal brands to consider:

Dr Jason Fox: He is a specialist in helping organisations think creatively about work. Dr Jason Fox has a fabulous brand: the playful professor. He makes jokes from the stage about being an introvert, he is fairly casual in his presentation style, and has a quirky look. In every way he epitomises his message of being authentic, creative, and fun in the quest to do good work. www.drjasonfox.com

The Queen: In radical contrast, the British Queen is the epitome of her brand: service. She is quiet and stoic in word and deed. She dresses with dignity and simplicity, and when required, in pomp for ceremony. Everything about her radiates grace and stewardship.

Lorna Jane Clarkson: Active wear Aussie entrepreneur, Lorna Jane has her brand infused in all aspects of her company. She personally models an active lifestyle by exercising every day, eating well, and maintaining a healthy, active body. Her entire message springs from her personal purpose of encouraging women to have active, healthy lives. It's one of the reasons her stores are so successful, with 155 stores worldwide. www.lornajane.com.au

...and me! My personal brand is filtered by adventure and authenticity. Whether I am presenting in a corporate boardroom or facilitating a program in the wilds of Western Australia, I bring adventure and fun to my approach. I wear a little silver hiking boot to remind me of past and future adventures and keep that spirit of excitement ignited. In my corporate facilitator kit I have Osho Zen tarot cards, Tibetan cymbals to call the class to order, and a rubber chicken. Every good facilitator needs a rubber chicken!

Once we have our coat of arms, our personal brand, we can then seek to amplify our inner resilience. We will need courage and strength on our quest, should we encounter perils, dragons, and miscreants. We can seek help, through guidance of archetypal figures.

Leveraging archetypes for the quest

On any quest we need guidance and resources to help us grow and learn as leaders. In ancient times, archetypes were personified as Gods and Goddesses. Throughout literature they are recognisable character types such as hero and villain.

Archetypes provide us with the opportunity to achieve harmony and resonance with our shadow side. Our shadow is the least noble part of us. It is the part of us that harbours feelings like jealousy, rage, resentment. It is the destructive, combative, and dark side of ourselves. Mostly the shadow exists as a latent force. Accessing archetypes helps us to harmonise the shadow side with our strong side so we remain balanced and on track.

Exploring these archetypes also allows us to create synergies. This is when two seemingly competing energies create a complimentary relationship that is greater than the sum of its parts. Joseph Campbell outlines various archetypal figures in his work, as do other writers such as Carol Pearson and Carl Jung in his psychology treatises.

With archetypes in leadership presence, we want to move from the alpha (usually alpha male) concept of leadership to one that is integrated. In particular, we want to balance the male and female energies inherent in leadership presence.

Like a good marriage, the strengths of one are complimented by the strengths of the other. Integrated leadership archetype energies are like the perfect marriage.

There are three realms of archetypes, which we can apply to integrate into our leadership style:

1. Wisdom: Crone and Sage

The Crone is an archetypal figure; an elderly figure like the wise woman, and also a protective figure. Her shadow side is cantankerous and obstructive.

The Crone's male counterpart is the Sage. The Sage is the wise old man, a father-like figure who dispenses advice to younger travellers/ heroes to help them become more of who they are. Sometimes the Sage is represented as a wizard or hermit. The shadow side is seen as a devouring father (Cronus) or a doddering absent-minded fool.

Balancing the two archetypes is about integrating the guardian energy of the Crone and the instructive energy of the Sage while accepting and managing the shadow side of both.

2. Compassion: Mother and Father

The Mother archetype represents caring and nurturing: a sustaining and supportive energy. Her shadow side is devouring, seducing and poisonous. This has also been known as 'smother'.

The Father archetype represents law, order, and discipline. The shadow side emerges when protection turns into abuse of authority. It can be controlling, rigid, and overly intellectual. An inflated sense of hubris is also a hallmark of the shadow father archetype.

A balance of the positive aspects of Mother and Father creates supportive environments that nurture and strengthen without being overly directive or controlling.

3. Governance: Queen and King

Both the King and Queen represent authority, structure, and guidance.

The Queen represents service, elegance, and grace. The true qualities of the Queen are related to a gentle use of power and authority. She is in service to the realm, leading with grace, care, and concern. Her shadow side emerges as arrogance, jealousy, and defensiveness.

The King represents protection, stability, and order. He is often pictured as the center of existence, the benevolent protective figure. His shadow side is the tyrant and weakling.

How can we use these archetypes to amplify our leadership presence?

When balanced compassion (Mother and Father) blends with balanced governance (King and Queen), the result is *resilience* in leadership.

When balanced wisdom energy (Crone and the Sage), blends with balanced governance (King and Queen), this creates *expansion* in leadership.

When balanced compassion (mother and father) blends with balanced wisdom energy (Crone and the Sage), this creates *transcendence.* Wise counsel and compassionate support allow us to move past ego concerns into egoless growth and adventure.

Key tips to balancing these archetypes:

In your reflection practice, check how each of the following archetypes are being expressed:

1. Wisdom
- Crone: Am I guarding without being obstructive?
- Sage: Am I instructive without being over-bearing? Am I helpful or too distant?

2. Compassion
- Mother: Am I nurturing without smothering?
- Father: Am I protecting without controlling?

3. Governance
- Queen: Am I serving without arrogance or jealousy?
- King: Am I ruling without being a tyrant?

Through balancing archetypes, individuals and their teams can grow safely within the boundaries and structures set by the balanced leader.

Mapping the quest

Now that we have plans and archetypes to guide our path, we need a map to follow for the adventure. There will be many mountains to climb, treasures to discover, and chasms to avoid.

This quest map is for personal growth. In our growth as leaders, we need to focus on internal as well as external aspects of our development. By mapping these, we focus our activity towards improvement.

We choose our own Everest. We can choose epic challenges in our personal and professional world. For some, this may be learning to tango. For others, this may be learning a new language. Other examples are traveling to a new country, going on a weekend camping expedition in the wilderness, or writing a book.

External mountains

External 'mountains' are specific skills or capacities. Ones related to leadership are things like:

- Strategic thinking capacity such as foresight, trend analysis, systems thinking
- Creative solution-finding ability such as mind-mapping, customer experience mapping, brainstorming, idea generation
- Team engagement skills such as creating safety, building team lore, establishing and maintaining a robust culture
- Scenario planning
- Presentation skills
- Communication finesse.

These are the leader's tools and need to be honed, sharpened and polished like any instrument for a craft. We can pick a specific challenge in one of these areas to focus on each quarter. For example, we might pick 'refine presentation skills'. We can then map our plan to do this by attending a workshop, delivering three presentations, and asking for specific feedback on elements of our presentation.

Internal mountains

Internal 'mountains' are about self-mastery. They include physical prowess and resilience, mental focus, emotional intelligence, spiritual awareness, and intuitive abilities.

In *Unbeatable Mind*, Mark Divine calls these the Five Mountains. As a US Navy SEAL, Divine crafted a training program for civilians and SEAL candidates that engaged all five mountains in his regime.

In the Five Mountains, every training day is an opportunity to hone physical capacity in strength, endurance, flexibility, stamina as well as mental focus, emotional resilience and positive thinking, spiritual purpose, and intuitive sharpness. His protocols include breath training, visualisation, journaling, connection to purpose, and integrating these into any physical activity. This kind of integrated approach to development is crucial to the success of elite warriors like US Navy SEALs, who must perform in the most arduous of conditions.

Not all of us seek to be warriors with genuine weapons. However, each of us has within us a warrior spirit. Each of us seeks to protect and further the cause of what we hold most dear. Adopting the warrior discipline of the Five Mountains is a great way to become centered, integrated, and aligned to what matters most.

From politicians to business leaders and community leaders, we all need to choose a mountain challenge to explore thresholds and expand our capacity for contribution. Every leader needs to have their own development as a key priority. Those who don't aren't growing, and they're holding themselves, their teams, and their organisations back.

Some examples of internal mountains are:

- Develop a journaling practice to plan and review the day
- Practice meditation to learn focus and concentration skills
- Do breath training to learn to control arousal response
- Practice yoga for concentration and integrated mind-body connection
- Learn body awareness to develop intuition
- Read about different religious faiths to expand spiritual awareness
- Use visualisation to develop focus on purpose and goal orientation.

INSIGHT

Planning my own growth

Personal growth has always been tremendously important to me. Every year I choose something new to learn from the Five Mountains. One year it was a mountaineering course in New Zealand, another year it was belly dancing, and another year, meditation.

This year I'm embracing *Kokoro* spirit. This Japanese word literally translates to 'heart', though its meaning broadens to 'the heart of things'. To me it is the alignment of word, action, deed, and heart. Everything I do is aligned in service to my higher purpose of helping leaders be more wise, compassionate, and centered.

I've now adopted some of Divine's practices as my own. I journal each morning and evening, I connect my plans to purpose, and visualise workouts as a spiritual as well as physical practice. I have specific goals on my learning map to keep me focused. Some examples are to do a personal best in a 10km fun run, to complete 20 pull-ups in two minutes, and to undertake a meditation retreat.

Being at my best physically, mentally, emotionally helps me connect spiritually and to enhance my intuitive self. All this enables me to serve my purpose and message better.

Growth and service start with a plan.

Key points for focus

Prepare quest plans

- Lifetime and legacy vision, the Big Why
- 20-year blocks with feeling theme words
- Current decade theme word
- Current one-year plan: theme word, holidays, experiences, people to spend time with, what to learn, how to beautify the home, internal and external mountains
- 90-day projects
- Weekly plans
- Daily plans.

Develop the coat of arms – brand

Imagine a trusted colleague talking about your personality, talent, and capability. What do you want to be known for? Do your behaviour and attitude align with this?

Use archetypes to help guide development and focus

Build in wisdom, compassion, and governance to focus with your reflection practice.

Map the quest to the mountains

Choose challenges to include in the one-year, quarterly, weekly and daily plans.

External mountains: Identify leadership skills and capacities that need to be developed.

Internal mountains: Choose mental, physical, emotional, spiritual, and intuitional skills to hone.

The Crucible
In The Dragon's Lair

When we dare the dragon, we need to summon courage, resolve, and focused intention to overcome what looms as a threat. As leaders, we need to know how to do this for ourselves first. And then we take our team with us – into the heart of the crucible.

Learning how to resolve our deepest personal challenges is the first crucible. When we can do that, we can then hold the space for others to undergo their own crucible experiences. As centered leaders we can lead our team through our collective challenges. Whether it's an industry crisis like the collapse of the Chinese mineral market, an organisational re-structure, or a family health threat, we can get through it and be stronger for it. This is the essence of mastering the dragon's crucible.

The dragon's crucible

As leaders, we undergo our own experiences in the crucible during the course of our journey. We stand before the dragon in a crucible heated by the flames of its breath, scorched, scalded, and ultimately transformed.

I experienced my major brush with the dragon's crucible in 2005. I was diagnosed with cancer, and plunged head-first into the crucible.

Afterwards, I discovered that since I knew that I could challenge the biggest dragon and come out whole again, I could do that for others. I could hold that space for clients, colleagues, friends, and family – I could be the crucible for them so they too might be transformed.

INSIGHT

Full immersion in the crucible

When I was told I had cancer, the earth tilted. I slid into a deep, dark cave and there I found the red-eyed dragon waiting for me.

My body had betrayed me. I saw it as a separate entity, one I had to deal with only begrudgingly: feed it, rest it, trot it out for exercise. I saw it as an obstacle to overcome, in spite of my physical limitations. It was no wonder that I was ill. That year I had had eight colds and flus. I was treating my body as an enemy instead of an ally.

I had major abdominal surgery to remove the cervical cancer; quite an advanced, aggressive tumour. They discovered it had spread to my lymph nodes, and this meant chemotherapy to poison any traces of the cancer cells. Through my chemotherapy treatments, I was scalded from the inside out. Cisplatin is a platinum derivative so toxic that the nurses had to wear eye protection and thick rubber gloves to hook it up to my IV. The process took a whole day while I was attached to a drip, flushing my body with saline, then with the Cisplatin, and then another flush of saline. I was green and grey at the end of the day, swimming with chemicals and a foul metal taste in my mouth.

The chemo cave was a silent, cold, and lonely place. None of my fellow cancer patients spoke to each other. Some looked better than others. Some had hair, some didn't. Some looked busy and focused, others stared glassy-eyed out the window.

Alone at home, letting the chemicals wash through me, I sat with my journal. It was time to meet the dragon once more. I stepped into my journal and it was a full immersion in the dragon's crucible. I poured out all my deepest fears, deepest regrets, and let them scourge and punish me. I turned to look at all the past wrongs done to me, all the shameful mistakes I'd made in relationships, all the self-loathing I'd allowed myself to wallow in: too fat, too scared, too weak, too bitchy.

I finally owned up to my own shadow, my own demons, and gave them a long wailing voice. And when the tears ended and my writing was exhausted, I slumped in my chair. I felt the embers of the crucible burn low, smoulder, and die out.

I'd survived.

Leaving the cave was a long journey. My physical healing took a good couple of years before I claimed full energy once more.

My spiritual and emotional journey began in earnest. I made deliberate decisions to look after myself, to be kinder to myself. I raised my standards of self-care, strengthened boundaries around my time and activities, and turned the mirror inward to examine and cleanse my internal dialogue.

The secret elixir I had discovered in my tangle with the dragon was that I was in charge of my life. I was captain of my own ship, I could chart my own course, and I could live in faith, not fear.

I renewed my conviction for making a contribution. If I could survive, others could too. I wanted to ensure that what I learned in the fiery depths could be passed on to others. I realised that who I was as a leader, how I held myself, and how I connected to others created both the model and the space for others to achieve their own transformation.

Key skills for helping others through their crucible moments

As an executive coach, friend, and family member, these are the paradigms and frameworks I use to help others find their path through challenge.

1. **Use compassion and wisdom in the interaction.**
   Compassion is the best of the heart while wisdom is best of the mind. When we are deeply compassionate, we show the

other person deep love and caring. When we are wise, we help them to help themselves.

2. **Hold the other person as powerful.** Even if the other person feels they are helpless and stuck, see them as strong. If we believe they can make decisions for themselves and own their life experience, then we carry a seed of possibility for them. It also helps us from getting dragged in to the drama of their story. This helps us to stay focused on the path forward rather than the murky quagmire of the current situation.

3. **Know they will be ok.** This is one of the hardest attitudes to embrace, especially if it is someone we care about. We don't like to see our loved ones suffer. Taking a spiritual approach, or a higher level of faith is helpful here. For me, one of my beliefs is that we all return to source energy after death. So death is just a transition. The grief and anxiety I feel when someone I love is ill or dying is two-fold: I feel empathy for their plight and I will miss them if they pass on. Knowing that my grief is ok helps. Knowing they will be ok helps more.

4. **Keep an image of them fully healed, strong and successful.** Regardless of what the other person is currently facing, or whether they believe they will be successful or not, I carry that belief for them and tell them so. For example, I had one client who endured months of toxic engagements with her supervisor. She felt trapped and beholden to the organisation. She wanted to stay and try and make things work, yet this became more difficult as the conflict escalated. She felt truly helpless through it all. I kept reminding her that I saw her as strong and deserving of a workplace that acknowledged her talent and contribution. I emphasised that I knew somehow she would make it through and experience the professional success she longed for. She went through a dispute resolution process that ended with a severance package. She is now taking maternity leave and cultivating her own highly successful consultancy practice. She is deeply happy and fulfilled.

5. **Guide them with questions, not solutions.** As leaders we sometimes want to jump in with a quick fix solution. The

answer seems obvious! A key responsibility as centered leaders however is to grow other centered leaders. When we teach others to think constructively for themselves, we have given them tools to feel autonomous again. Some key questions to foster proactivity are:

- 'What do you want instead?'
- 'What did you do to contribute to this situation?'
- 'What can you learn from this?'
- 'What might be good about this?'
- 'What's the first step you can take to move forward?'

6. **Drop judgement.** It is very easy to make judgements about the other person's choices, attitude, and circumstances. I find this is especially true of family members! We can heap judgement on those closest to us. We think it's being 'caring', but really it is condescension. We imagine what we would do in their situation and find our choices would be 'better'. Again, this is about letting the other person have their own life experience and to support them with love.

7. **Be responsible to and not for them.** This is a helpful paradigm for centered leaders. It means that we are *responsible to* others for how we show up, our attitude, our thinking, our compassion. We are not however *responsible for* the other person's decisions, choices, or even outcomes. They need to own that. We own how we serve as a support as they go through their crucible experience.

8. **Detach from the outcome.** This is easily said and difficult to embrace. We hold positive thoughts and good intentions for others and we want to see them happy and fulfilled in their own experiences. If we get attached to the outcomes we envision, we are heaping expectations on the decision they may or may not make. This creates pressure neither of us need. We need to go back to trusting the process will be ok in the end, regardless of the choices they make, especially if it's not something we might have chosen for ourselves.

As an example, in my own experience I made a difficult choice to leave an organisation I loved because I felt it was destructive for me and holding me back. It took me a long time to make the decision, but when I did, my Universe exploded in possibilities and positive experiences. I realised I should have made that choice much sooner.

When I encounter someone who is struggling with something similar, I feel the powerful surge of wanting it to be better for them too, knowing how painful it can be. It's tempting to get caught up as an evangelist for a certain type of action, and to heap that on others. This is much like the overbearing enthusiasm of reformed smokers against their still-smoking counterparts. Ironically, this kind of encouragement often backfires. People want to make their own choices, and will live, or die, by their outcomes.

If we hear ourselves saying, "If only they would ....", then we know we are getting attached to outcomes and marching towards preaching rather than encouraging.

9. **They don't need rescuing.** This can feel wrong at times. When we see someone who is truly suffering, the natural human tendency is to want to end the pain. If we do this for them, we deny them the chance to grow from the experience.

Judgement is of course required in this principle. This is where we often struggle. If someone clearly has a challenge, such as financial one, and we know that if we gave them some money it would fix the current situation, then what do we do? Will they learn and carry on from strength to strength? Or will they repeat the mistake *ad infinitum*, especially if we are there as the fall back? It is a classical ethical dilemma with no hard and fast answers. If we hold them as powerful, however, and start with the premise they don't need rescuing, then we find we may be able to work through the challenge with them so they find their own answers.

10. **Each of us has a soul contract to fulfil.** I find this is a helpful paradigm to detach from other people's drama and avoid compassion fatigue. From a spiritual perspective, if we see each of us on a spiritual journey in a physical body, then what happens to us, no matter how terrible, serves our growth and learning on the journey. This helps us to make peace with what is happening, while able to offer assistance and support.

11. **Pray.** Prayer is a connection to spirit, however we envision and represent that. It's not a prayer to fix problems or make

Composure

things better, it's a prayer to find strength and courage to live through the crucible and find something meaningful in it. When we do that for ourselves as well as others, we surrender to the path as a way of moving forward.

INSIGHT

Being present and holding the space for others

When I got the call from my sister, I knew I had to go. My Dad had been wheeled into emergency surgery and was facing multiple organ failure. His 'routine' bowel cancer surgery had not gone according to plan: part of his bowel had died with a pinched blood vessel and the tissue had come apart, leaking the contents of his bowels into his abdominal captivity. He was filling up with poison from his own body.

It was a long trip from Australia, through New York and onwards to tiny Prince Edward Island. Forty hours of travel, not knowing if I was going home for a funeral, a vigil, or both.

My brother and sisters arrived too, and together with our Mum, we waited. Dad came out of surgery in an induced coma, on a ventilator, sprouting a fountain of tubes. He was rigged to a panel of display monitors, his chest heaving and his heart rate pounding as his body laboured through the crisis of surgery. They had to flush his abdomen multiple times, pulling apart the intestines as they were fused together by the acid in the bowel fluids.

It was grim. One of the island's vicious snowstorms raged, and we were marooned in the hospital. We tried to sleep in the cramped waiting room in Intensive Care. The time was punctuated by nurse visits and checks by the doctor. They repeated the rinse out operation three more times before sewing him up, fingers crossed against infection.

They woke Dad from the induced coma, though he could not speak as the ventilator was still in place. My siblings left the day before the ventilator was removed. I stayed to help my Mum, and spend Christmas with her, and hopefully Dad.

I sat with my mother and held her in my heart as I watched her stand in a deep pit of black unknown, facing the loss of her life partner, the demise of her life as she knew it, an end to the passionate hobby of house renovations (impossible without the financial and physical support of my Dad), and sense of purpose. The emotions ranged from stunned shock, to despair, to horror, to anger and frustration. She told me to 'eff off' a couple of times. I felt her emotion thunder and crash all around me.

I stood in the deep pit with her, holding the space for grief and fear to have its due. I reassured her we could make it through this, whatever 'this' turned out to be. I helped create a calm anchor in the eye of the storm.

A few days after the last surgery, they removed the ventilator, and we heard Dad speak. Glorious! He was moved a day or so later out of Intensive Care, and in to recovery. After nine days in a coma and four surgeries, he was alive, and making incremental progress. He had lost 17kg (35 pounds), could barely move his arms, and could only sit for an hour before tiring. Two months of intensive rehabilitation in hospital were ahead of him.

A few days after the last surgery, they removed the ventilator, and we heard Dad speak. Glorious! He was moved a day or so later out of Intensive Care, and in to recovery. After nine days in a coma and four surgeries, he was alive, and making incremental progress. He had lost 17kg (35 pounds), could barely move his arms, and could only sit for an hour before tiring. Two months of intensive rehabilitation in hospital were ahead of him.

We celebrated Christmas at his hospital bedside the day they removed the last feeding tube. We toasted life and Christmas in red plastic wine cups. Never had I felt more grateful than that day.

I left my Mum a few days later to head back to Australia. As I hugged her and felt her tired, drawn, shrunken shoulders,

I reached for the thought that she would be all right. I kept thinking, 'All will be well', though it did not seem so at the time.

On the long plane ride across the ocean, I wept.

Composure

I think my ability to stay centered in this crisis has evolved from doing deep emotional work. Accepting intense feelings, allowing them, and letting them go.

It also comes from a deeper connection to spirit, and a world view that holds us all as deeply connected, and each of us a powerful human being having our own special life adventure. I worked to release the sense of responsibility for my parents, choosing to be responsible *to* them instead of *for* them. I didn't need to rescue them, just to be there to guide them gently to find their own path forward.

Crucible experiences with our teams

Guiding our teams through crucible moments has a few more complex layers. As leaders, when we take our team toe-to-toe with a dragon, we can *create* and *maintain* the space for crucible transformation, *collaborate* within that space, and then *hold* the space.

1. Commanding: Creating belonging

To create a space for crucible experiences, we need to develop command. This is about attraction and stewardship, of a group, team, community: the tribe. Command is all about care of the soul and spirit of the group. It's the ability to touch and ignite the inner world of one's tribe members. How we foster soul and belonging in our tribe and teams allows others to excel individually and collectively.

When I arrived in Australia in 1996, I joined Outward Bound. When I walked in to the morning meeting room and saw a sea of people in fleece jumpers and hiking boots, I thought, "This is my tribe!"

At last I was among like-minded people who knew the joy of sleeping under the stars, the exhilaration of physical challenge rewarded with mesmerising views, and the strange quirky banter that emerges with companions in the bush. We even dressed the same: ready for adventure!

More than adventure and a love of wilderness there was a sense of belonging, of being part of something bigger than me. Something meaningful, that did good in the world, for people and planet.

This is, after all, what we all long for.

As leaders we have a core responsibility to create that sense of belonging and purpose, for ourselves, and for the people who claim us as their tribe.

Seth Godin, in his fantastic book *Tribes*, says: "There are tribes everywhere now, inside and outside of organizations, in public and in private, in nonprofits, in classrooms, across the planet. Every one of these tribes is yearning for leadership and connection."

As leaders, we need to call the tribe together. Offer members an opportunity to connect – with us, with each other, and with the Big Idea or purpose. When I was at Outward Bound, the Big Idea was to help individuals discover more of who they are in places so beautiful you couldn't help but be uplifted and inspired by the endless rugged awe of the wilderness.

Today I still claim that Big Idea as one of my central purposes: to reveal to people their inner genius. I have now focused that around doing good in and for the world. I gather leaders around me who are committed to taking on the world's challenges, transforming them into opportunities, healing the world's wounds, and unleashing creative ideas to craft new prosperity and abundance for all of us.

One of our role as leaders is to help our team members feel connected to and focused on the sense of purpose, the 'why' of the work. Without daily connection to the cause or purpose, enthusiasm and engagement may wane.

A sense of team belonging does not develop on its own. Like a garden, team belonging needs maintenance, care, and attention. As a leader, we must create safety, leverage our team's unique talents, and also manage their differences.

1. Create safety

It all starts with creating safety in the group. When people feel comfortable in a group, it meets a profound and primal need to belong. Our ancestors roamed about in furs and gathered in caves together because it was safer in a group to fend off marauding flesh-eating nasties and other rival tribes than to go it alone.

Creating safety in a group is much more subtle than simply shoving a group of people together in some office cave and dubbing them members of the 'fill in the blank' team. Creating safety requires strong commitment from the leader. The fundamentals of creating team safety include:

- *Setting boundaries and guidelines for group behaviour.* This identifies what is acceptable behaviour and what is not. For example, it's ok to praise Susie publicly for her diligent work and buy her a doughnut, but it's not ok to make fun of George for his body odour and tuna snacks. Or: it's ok to take time away from work for the occasional family commitment such as a school play, but it is not ok to consistently arrive 30 minutes late.

- *Celebrating the truth tellers.* These are the courageous ones who dare to speak up against the status quo, who ask the difficult questions about a process or decision, and who query long-held practices that seem out of place. Truth tellers shed light on golden nuggets that may create breakthroughs or prevent disaster. Truth can be uncomfortable, and possibly not very popular. This is all the more reason to celebrate truth tellers for their courage! Truth is one person's perspective, but sometimes that perspective is the part we can't see. It's like the bald patch at the back of our head. It hurts to be shown, but if we don't know about it, we can't do anything about it.

- *Getting to know team members as individuals.* When we come to know our team members as humans, a sense of trust and belonging results. Our team feels acknowledged as individuals, not cogs in a machine. When the leader takes time – both individually and with the team – to explore individual stories, things they care about, things they like and don't like, are excited about, afraid of, and hope for, a little bloom of delight appears on the souls of our colleagues. The work becomes more enjoyable because we know others care about us. We develop a sense of belonging.

- *De-stigmatising failure.* Avoidance of failure can lead to stymied team performance. If the team members associate failure with disapproval, or worse, things like demotion or rejection, then the focus becomes risk-avoidance and covering up errors. Creativity and innovation are hampered. As leaders we need to model this religiously. We need to own up to mistakes and focus on what we can be learned from them. If we preach the attitude, 'It's not a mistake unless we don't learn from it', then we will embrace a learning and growth attitude.

2. Leverage talent

I had my biggest breakthrough as a leader when I learned that people thought differently to me, preferred to work differently to me, and that my way was not always the best way.

Numerous profiling tools can assist with understanding the team's natural style and working strengths. There is DiSC, a behaviour profiling instrument, or the Myers-Briggs Type Indicator that looks at personality architecture, amongst many others. These tools offer insight into individual preferences as well as the effect on team dynamics.

Armed with this knowledge, we can create projects and duties that bring out the best of existing strengths, as well a focus on development plans that suit the individual.

Knowing our teammates' behaviour preferences and strengths gives us secret insider magic to make the most of these, so our team is robust and thriving.

3. Manage difference

As soon as there are two or more sets of eyes, ears, and mouths in one place, we will have differences of opinion. As leaders, we need to manage that difference. It can be a beautiful thing, when we do it right. Difference can be a source of enlightenment.

Managing differences of opinion can be done well if we've laid the groundwork beforehand. Through establishing clear ground rules, we can acknowledge that every person's opinion is valuable and that truth telling is sacrosanct. It's also important not to set the expectation that just because an opinion is shared means that it will be adopted.

In healthy teams, difference of opinion leads to new ideas. Contrasting arguments allow for new perspective and new insight.

When safety, talent, and difference are managed well, the team dynamic evolves into a cohesive, synergistic experience.

Sweet spot #1: When we create safety and leverage talent, we get *engagement*. People feel secure in their work. Their best talents and preferences are used effectively and they are free to excel and perform.

Sweet spot #2: When we leverage talent and manage difference, we get *collaboration*. Individuals feel valued for their skills and talents and are recognised for their unique perspective. They will want to share and develop ideas with their colleagues.

Sweet spot #3: When we manage difference and create safety, we get *innovation*. This means that individuals feel safe to share their ideas, no matter how unusual or difficult. From here ideas can grow organically amongst team members.

At the epicentre of this dynamic, we have trust, honesty, and respect. This creates the golden elixir of leadership – oxytocin. Oxytocin is the feel-good hormone that occurs during breastfeeding, and also in well-bonded teams. It is the currency of synergistic team cultures.

LEADER FOCUS: Colin Hendrie

Leading a team through the crucible of war

Colin Hendrie is a former Major in the Rhodesian (now Zimbabwe) Army who saw plenty of live action. He went on to serve as Raaid (Major) in the Sultan's special forces of Oman. Colin is the type of leader who can inspire others to great feats of courage, even in the face of torture and death. What is it about Col that is so compelling?

Physically he lacks the assets attributed to influential leaders: he is short, round, and losing hair. Now in his 60s, he walks with a pronounced limp. This is the man many hold in reverence, deep affection and love.

Col is at once self-effacing and flattering. He has a dry wit and an ice-blue gaze that would freeze over hell. He has nerves of steel and composure in the most grating of circumstances. He is a natural storyteller, holding court to spell-bound groups with tales of past programs, scoundrels, adventures, heroes, and villains he has known.

Now he is one of Australia's most respected experiential educators in outdoor adventure, particularly in Western Australia and the Kimberley region. His company Outback Initiatives was established over 20 years ago, and he has overseen development programs for many of Australia's biggest coal mining and corporate organisations, as well as for the Gurkha Contingent in the Singaporean Police Force, and Prison staff. Col is a renowned specialist in team development, and teaches others to lead with grace under literal and metaphoric fire.

Colin's story reaches deep in to our consciousness with its stark pain and gripping humanity.

Born in Africa, his mother died in suspicious circumstances when he was just a boy of nine. The stepmother who moved in shortly after drove him to escape into the bush, where he sojourned with snakes, lions, and other beasts. The bush became not only his sanctuary but also a vast adventure playground where he learned self-reliance and solace in the marvels of the natural world.

As soon as he was old enough Colin joined the military. There he quickly earned a reputation for being a challenge to authority. On the receiving end of many cruel punishments, Colin developed a deep disdain for leadership expressed as power and control. Despite being a troublemaker, Colin progressed through the ranks and grew a command for himself. His men loved him. He did not set himself above them, but treated them with infinite respect and consideration. He was one of them.

Colin says of military hierarchy: "I thought a lot of it was bullshit. In officer training they taught you to lead through fear. I always thought that was a mistake. I worked under a man like that for a while. He took great pleasure in punishing people for the smallest of offences. By God he was cruel! An officer like

Composure

that was always at risk of 'friendly fire'. If it came to it and there was an opportunity for a stray bullet to be 'mis-aimed' during a skirmish, then there would have been a few who might have been tempted. And none would have said a word."

Colin's approach is a stark contrast. He treats others with courtesy, friendliness, and respect. He sees others as equals, regardless of rank, experience or background.

Colin's leadership philosophy boils down to courage and compassion.

Courage when the stakes are high

Moving into the special forces, Colin and his crew saw plenty of live action. Captured by the enemy and threatened with execution by firing squad, Colin taunted his captors and dared them to follow through. He knew the rebels would not dare kill him for fear of consequences. Colin was too well respected on both sides of the conflict.

Colin tells the story of being on a stakeout, right against enemy lines. As he was lying in the grass, he became aware of one of the enemy just ten metres away. As if in slow motion, he remembers reaching for his rifle and shouldering it, looking through the viewfinder at the whites of the enemy's eyes as he did the same. Then he pulled the trigger. Col survived; the enemy did not.

When I asked him what he thought of killing people when he was in the army, he describes it like this: "When I joined I thought it was a lark and great fun, like playing Cowboys and Indians. We had a duty to do, and we did our job. Have I killed people? Yes I have, it was part of the job. Us or them. But one thing that my experience in the military has taught me is that war is absolutely senseless. It's the biggest waste of human life and human potential. The world does not need more wars. It needs more people to speak the truth."

And this is where I started to get a window in to Colin's soul, and the energy that sweeps up his colleagues, participants, and friends in rapturous awe.

Compassion through the crucible

Here is a man who has known enormous pain and trauma in his childhood and overcome it through communion with the natural world; touching the creation of the universal mind in his effort to be comforted.

Here is a man who then went on to live between the lines of life and death, where life can be snuffed by chance and winners are determined by whimsy and politics. To have killed and nearly been killed sharpened his zest for life and living, rooted in a deep knowingness of the fleetingness of it all.

Having seen and experienced what he has, this is still not what binds people to Colin Hendrie. His charisma is considerable, his gravitas unequalled, his storytelling mesmerising.

These aspects of his presence are like the sauce on the steak: the real meat of Colin Hendrie's presence is in his heartfelt love of people.

Colin eventually left the military. He joined the corporate world and excelled in his ability to build engagement. He knew how to talk with people, to listen, and to care. He took this and applied it to his educational business because he knew one thing: people are everything.

This is what people feel in Colin Hendrie's presence. They feel his deep connection, care, and concern for them as human beings, each a rare and unique creation of the universe. You can feel his compassion, his interest, and his unfeigned admiration and support.

On his leadership programs, Colin sets the requirement that people 'speak the truth'. He acknowledges that this is not always easy, and as leaders we can shy away of speaking the difficult truths because we are afraid of what others may think, how others may feel, or how we might be perceived. But Colin believes that if more truth was spoken there would be less war, less trouble, and more opportunity to connect rather than divide.

And as we listen to him, something deep within us resonates, like a deep and distant chord of our heartstrings. He calls us to be better, to have courage, to uplift, to trust and have faith in humanity by being more human.

From someone who has been to the edge of hell and who has seen the darkest corners of the human soul, we feel it in every cell as a message from a living celestial messenger made incarnate.

Yet Col is hardly a deity or an angel.

Perhaps this is why we are so drawn to him. Col can be pig-headed, stubborn, and task-driven at a rate of knots that is difficult to keep up with. He is easily swayed by others' opinions and once crossed, he tends to judge that person with a tarnished and unforgivable brush.

He speaks an elevated message from a broken and healed platform. We see his weaknesses and this helps us to forgive our own. We see his weaknesses and acknowledge a man still trying to do good in the world in spite of them. We see that even with faults, we can still make a positive difference. His determination and will give strength to our own.

Key skills for creating team belonging

1. **Embrace others as equals.** Leadership is more than a title, it's a stewardship role for peers. There may be hierarchy and positional authority, but at the core we are all human beings. Starting with this in mind builds rapport and connection.

2. **Ask about them as people.** Our team mates are human beings with likes, dislikes, and aspirations. When we take the trouble to find out, we show we care. Tasks don't get done without people. An investment of interest in our people will build commitment to the task and purpose later.

3. **Identify the group's values, purpose, and expected behaviour.** When we make these explicit we build common ground quickly. We also create clear expectations that make it easier to address differences of opinions or behaviour misalignment.

4. **Create safety in the group.** As discussed previously, this means setting clear boundaries, encouraging speaking the truth, and modelling learning from failure.

5. **Create a sense of team identity.** This might be a team name, a uniform, a ritual group move (akin to football group hugs) or a team song. Displaying a photo of the group is a simple way to acknowledge the team.

6. **Build cultural lore.** When teams share adventure together, it builds a common story and strengthens connection between people. This is why team development in the outdoors is still one of the most powerful ways to build team engagement and cohesiveness. Less adventurous events serve a similar purpose: social events, excursions, and retreats.

7. **Show appreciation.** Appreciation between team members is a sign of love and respect between the members. It is particularly significant when it comes from the leader. Focus from the person with positional authority heightens the sense of recognition, and this in turn encourages loyalty and commitment.

8. **Give positive and constructive feedback in a timely way.** We all like to know if we are doing a good job or not. When we as leaders make the effort to tell people, then this encourages others to keep putting in effort. When we give time feedback, it shows we care, that we're paying attention, and that we are committed to helping others grow and evolve.

9. **Create a habit of celebrating success.** This one often gets missed. We can get so caught up in achieving goal after goal that we forget to take stock and acknowledge our progress. This can lead to feeling disheartened and losing motivation. Regular celebration of success helps make the ride feel worthwhile and enjoyable.

Key signs there is a sense of belonging in a team

Members:

- Feel valued and appreciated
- Feel a sense of inclusion

- Are using their key talents
- Are developing and growing
- Like and trust each other
- Feel liked and trusted
- Have the opportunity to help others
- Can see the outcome and benefit of their work
- Achieve excellence and feel successful
- Have fun.

2. Collaboration: Conditions for creating team crucible moments

As leaders, we will face many significant challenges with our teams. Sometimes the only way around the dragon is through collaboration. Like Knights of the Round Table, we must band together to defeat the foe. Two amazing things happen when collaboration is done well: dragons are dodged, and teams are transformed. Collaboration becomes a crucible experience for the team. Shared experiences (especially in adversity) become catalysts for group cohesion as well as personal transformation.

INSIGHT

The Outward Bound 'opportunity'

When I was new to Outward Bound, the Human Resources Manager, Jacko, called on me for an 'opportunity'.

'Opportunities' were generally a euphemism for something unpleasant. The situation was intense: it was peak season, with all hands on deck. Office staff were out in the field as dozens of groups with hundreds of students were marching through the bush in different locations across the country. We crossed our fingers that there would be no emergencies, as our support resources were stretched already.

My 'opportunity' was to act as course coordinator and back up to a two-group program. I had never done either role before and had no idea where to start. I was not alone. Jacko was in it too.

He was balancing Human Resources, emergency support and on-call duties, as well as helping pack oranges for food drops.

Somehow we pulled through this experience by leaning on each other, problem-solving when confounded with shuffling resources and juggling timetables while supporting the instructors in the field. Late nights, early mornings, long drives, lots of coffee and gobbled chocolate, and the garrulous laughs of colleagues-become-lifelong-friends as we collaborated through a crazy time.

What I learned from Jacko is that there are critical aspects that need to be in place if collaboration (especially during times of high pressure) is to be effective.

Before collaboration, as leaders we need to ask ourselves:

- How strong is the oxytocin (the sense of trust and connection) in the group?
- Have we had repeated positive experiences?
- Do we have a rigorous practice of truth telling?
- Do we strictly adhere to values-based behaviour rules and expectations?
- Do people feel safe to share their opinions?
- Do I respect this person/people?
- Do I acknowledge they have something to offer that is different to me?
- Am I prepared to be wrong?
- What are my biases and preferences?
- Is my ego attached to the outcome?
- How connected am I to the purpose?
- Am I connected enough to the purpose to let go of the solution needing to come from me?
- Who's not at the table – and should they be there?

In collaboration between team members, there is a need to drop ego for the sake of the cause. This is difficult if any team members are immersed in an expert paradigm.

Composure

Integral leadership theory and what makes you an 'expert'

This theory evolved out of the work by Don Beck and Christopher Cowan in *Spiral Dynamics*, mentioned previously, as well as various works by Ken Wilber, Susanne Cook-Greuter, and Bill Torbert. Integral leadership theory explains the 'expert' stage of adult leadership development in a developmental context. The main premise that cuts across each of these works is that adults continue to evolve their thinking and action logic in response to life and social conditions.

The development of the 'expert' stage happens in careers as we deepen our expertise in a particular field through experience or study. Development of expertise is critical in all fields; without expertise development we would have no brain surgeons, no engineers, no architects, and no teachers. In short, we would have no professions and no evolution of knowledge.

The hallmark of the 'expert' stage of development is the ability to rise above others with our deep knowledge and experience. It is how we develop our sense of self-esteem and confidence. The more we know, the more confident we feel, the more we get recognised and progress in our professional lives.

There are limitations to the expert stage of development. We tend to see issues through a black and white lens; right versus wrong, good versus bad. We tend to have binary thinking as a result. We also tend to dismiss other people's opinions if we do not consider them appropriately credentialed in our own field, or in their particular field. We see expertise as a measure of credibility and value.

This thinking is the death knell of crucible collaboration for leaders and their teams.

If we are judging contributors based on their past expertise instead of valuing their ideas for their own sake, then we are blinding ourselves to their insight. Furthermore, we may end up unplugging the oxytocin through dismissiveness, judgement, sidelining, ignoring, or belittling contributions by others we perceive as 'not expert enough'.

As leaders we need to do vigorous 'expert mindset' hygiene. We need to ensure our own biases are firmly checked. We then need to model and make explicit the expectations of truth telling, contributions, encouraging multiple viewpoints, and cultivating ego-less collaboration.

3. Carriage: holding the crucible space

To hold the space, we need to harness our carriage. Carriage is our demeanour, both inner and outer.

Our inner demeanour is our focus and energy. When we are centered, we can reassure, encourage, and allow transformation to occur. Change need not be punitive. Centered leaders offer a more gentle, compassionate process for growth. This inner calm is amplified through our external demeanour.

Our external carriage is our physical presence; what we wear, how we move, how we speak. It is the packaging that amplifies our inner qualities. This matters. Our carriage is the first lens through which others see us. We need to adopt the carriage that inspires, reassures, and centers ourselves and our team.

Inner demeanour – focus and energy

When our presence is centered, we engage from a deep place of connection. We experience all beings as interrelated on an energy level. We experience others beyond the connections of a social system, by proximity, and values systems. There is no separation, only the one we imagine for the joy of the creative process. When we are centered, we experience our interactions with others as a co-creation of our shared experience. Though we perceive each other as separate entities by our limited physical senses, we are connected through consciousness and the energy that makes up all things.

So how does this kind of knowing help the individual leader?

If we define leadership as the process of growth and change for a common purpose, we can identify the leader as a deliberate creator and partner in achieving that common purpose. The leader's role is then at once deeply introspective and profoundly outward-focused in their connection to others.

As leaders, we hold the space as a crucible when we start to engage with others who are attracted to a similar vision and whose values resonate with our own. Others are attracted not only to the words and images of our vision, but to our energy, our vibration. As we tell the story of our vision and values, it creates an emotional response, or emotional frequencies. These act like radio signals. Those who are dialled in to the same 'channel' join in.

This is why it is so essential to be mindful of the stories we tell as leaders about what we want to achieve. For example, if we are constantly repeating how things are hard, difficult, and challenging, then we will attract people and experiences who resonate with those vibrations.

The other tension we as centered leaders need to hold is the tension between current reality and what we're moving towards. This is the ideal tension for collaborative co-creation. We accept our current situation, no matter how unpleasant, and we keep focused on what we are evolving towards. When we are not fighting or resisting our current situation, we have more energy for focusing on what's next. If we loathe our current reality, we end up in struggle. This makes the crucible experience harder than it needs to be. It is far better to accept what it is and create what's next.

Key skills for holding the softer crucible space for transformation:

1. **A continual and unrelenting attention to our own inner vibration.** This should be one of love, compassion, joy, and peace.

2. **A continual and unrelenting sense of compassion.** This is for others, and most especially for ourselves. We need to have compassion for ourselves first before we have any for others.

3. **A continual and unrelenting practice of self-love and self-appreciation.** We do this through positive self-talk, adequate sleep, rest, nutrition, and exercise.

4. **A deep sense of connection with others.** We feel this as the energy that flows between all living things.

5. **Tell empowering stories.** We create through the stories we tell. We attract others through our stories. If we want to be magnets to others who have a positive solution-focused attitude, we need to make sure our stories about our experience, purpose, and plans are positive and proactive.

6. **Maintain creative tension.** We need to ensure there is a 'pulling forward' sensation by appreciating where we are as an individual, group, organisation or community (even if it is unpleasant and uncomfortable), and anticipating happily the new state we are evolving towards. This is in sharp contrast to the need to defy current realities in order to create a new future. This is the hard way (a tougher crucible way) of creating change, and it takes a lot more energy and effort.

Centered leadership pathways offer a more peaceful way of experiencing change, and ones that build their own positive momentum. In this way leaders and their teams experience that the better it feels, the better it gets; the better it gets, the better it feels.

Outer demeanour – physicality

Imagine a grand ball in the late 1800s. The first thing the party-goers see is a horse-drawn carriage pulling up in the circular gravel drive. What gets noticed first is the energy of the horses and the quality and finishings of the carriage itself. Whoever alights will be favourably received as being the owner or passenger of such a lovely vehicle. We bask in the radiance of our trappings. This is what Robert Cialdini in his book *Influence* calls the 'halo effect'.

Our packaging: our clothes, jewellery, cars, possessions and our stance are like the horse-drawn carriage. They are what people notice first. If we want to leverage the halo effect to make a good impression, to draw people to our cause and to reassure them they are in safe hands, we need to do more than simply be centered. We need to broadcast our message through external trappings as well.

I call this practice the 'head-to-toe', which I've adopted from the check we do in outdoor activities. We check that everything is safe and in place. In abseiling for example, we start with the helmet on, fitted, and clipped in properly. Hair is tucked out of the way, no dangling earrings or necklaces to get caught on anything, shirts are tucked in, nothing in the pockets to fall out or get painfully trapped, harness done up and locked properly, pants tucked into socks and out of snagging reach, shoelaces done up firmly. Now you are ready for action!

The same applies to us in our leadership context. We need to bring conscious awareness to our packaging and presentation. Everything carries a message, and we want to make sure we are deliberate and intentional with that message.

In a Western, corporate setting, the head-to-toe check might look like this:

- Hair: clean, tidy, styled
- Skin: hydrated and cared for
- Cosmetics: age appropriate, subtle, and understated
- Decolletage: modest and covered, with minimal or no cleavage showing
- Jewellery: simple, as high quality as can be afforded
- Piercings: none that are distracting or outside of the norm
- Hands: nails neat and trim
- Clothes: fit, clean, in good repair, current style
- Shoes: polished, in good condition.

There is a scene in *Casino Royale* (2006) when James Bond is in discussion with the female love interest of the film, Vesper. She scans him head to toe for his taste and size so she can source appropriate clothing for the event they are to infiltrate later. She names each brand and quality of piece of clothing, and queries the watch: "Rolex?" He replies, "Omega". "Beautiful," she says.

This not-so-subtle product placement demonstrates that James Bond's brand is suave sophistication. The trappings of his appearance are carefully chosen to reflect his desired image. They are signals to his audience that he is a man of taste and quality, and that he ought to be treated as such.

Attention to appearance is not just for movie stars, but for all leaders. Some of our more visible leaders in positions of authority invest considerably in image consultants to get it right.

Former Australian Prime Minister John Howard was famous for his wildly bushy eyebrows. Then he was made more famous again when they were trimmed by his barber. Howard's public office ratings improved. Overlooking his eyebrows had sent the message, 'lack of attention to detail', as well as giving an air of 'Mad Hatter'. With eyebrows in check, Howard sought to demonstrate his thoughtful restraint and care.

Details matter.

As centered leaders we choose our appearance not to claim deference or to elevate ourselves above others, but to reassure and reinforce our message. We reassure our tribe that we are confident and capable through visual cues. We reinforce our message (be it corporate, casual, or inspired) with what we wear. We reflect the expectations of our followers that we are like them, that we too belong. We also reflect aspirational qualities for our team to latch on to. When we dress and move with confidence, then we encourage confidence.

Carriage: body language

How we hold ourselves also broadcasts particular signals. Body language helped us evolve as a species, enabling us to tell friend from foe in an instant.

Many of these signals are minute, sent and subconscious. It's important not to get preoccupied with 'mastering' body language to give the right impression. This is akin to micromanaging digestion: there is a lot going on outside of our control! Our job when it comes to digestion is to manage the inputs; the body does the rest. Our job when it comes to body language is to manage a few key signals; the body does the rest.

There is a small miracle when it comes to body language. When we change our physiology, we change our psychology. In other words, when we move differently, we feel different. And when we feel different, we radiate different subconscious cues to our audience.

In other words, if we want to look confident, we need to feel confident. If we want to feel confident, all we need to do is shift our body positioning.

Again, we can take a head-to-toe approach to manage our broadcast.

Head-to-toe

- Head: are we positively focused? Are we visualising success, engagement, a positive response? Lift the head, chin out. This gives the impression of confidence, strength and determination. Smile. All sorts of positive hormones are released when we smile. It is also the universal signal for friendliness.

- Eyes: gaze directly at people as we enter a room, and don't look down. Make sure this is culturally appropriate outside of Western countries.
- Hands: use open hands as a welcoming gesture, not buried in pockets or hidden behind the back.
- Handshake: firm, with a full palm.
- Feet: planted firmly on the ground. Send energy like tree roots through the feet to create a sense of grounding if feeling nervous.
- Movement: to attract attention, move forward, and then stop.

Amy Cuddy undertook some remarkable work on the influence of body language and shared it in her 2012 TED Global Talk[4]. In her experiments, her research subjects performed 'high power poses' and 'low power poses' before engaging in an intensive interview process to rate their suitability and perceived competence in the potential role.

'Power poses' are simply stances that connote power and positional influence. She calls one of them the Wonder Woman (or Superman) pose: feet apart, fists on hip, looking defiant and eagle-eyed. The victory pose is another. This is hands raised above the head as if conquering the world. The seated pose has feet on the desk, leaning back with hands behind the head. 'Low power poses' are slumped over, closed, and shrinking body positions.

Cuddy's research showed that just two minutes of undertaking a high power pose was enough to boost feel-good power hormones (high testosterone and low cortisol). Testosterone makes us feel strong and confident, and cortisol is an acute stress-response hormone.

After two minutes of posing she found through saliva testing of hormones that:

- Testosterone goes up 20% for high power posers; and
- Testosterone goes down 10% for low power posers.
- Cortisol decreases 25% for high power posers; and
- Cortisol increases 15% for low power posers.

---

4 Your Body Language Shapes Who You Are: http://www.ted.com/talks/amy_cuddy_your_body_language_shapes_who_you_are?language=en

In other words, the students who did power poses were more relaxed and confident than their low-power poser counterparts who were more stressed and less confident – *after just two minutes.*

As a result, in the experiment the role-playing interview panel recommended the power posers uniformly ahead of the low-power posers. Cuddy proved that our presence, when it is genuine and authentic, affects positively how we are received by others. Our personal presence emerges through the hormonal effect of the power poses. She proves that "Our bodies change our minds, our minds can change our behaviours, and our behaviours can change our outcomes."

If we pose confidently and feel confident, we are seen as confident. Our true selves get to shine.

Key points for contribution

- Develop key skills and mental frameworks for helping others through their crucible moments.

- To guide a team through crucible moments, first develop a deep sense of connection and belonging in the team.

- To build a collaborative atmosphere, drop the expert black-and-white thinking.

- Monitor inner demeanour to project confidence and inclusion.

- Do a head-to-toe check for inner and outer demeanour to check that attitude and packaging represent purpose and message.

Taming The Dragon
With Grace Under Fire

To have real grace under fire when the crucible heat is turned way up and the dragon is snorting and raging, we need to access our deep inner wisdom born of composed stillness, and our emotional agility. This is what I call 'Emotional Aikido'.

Aikido is described as the 'art of harmony'. It is a martial art practice that was developed from the battle technique to a path of spiritual development. The modern martial art practice was developed by Morihei Ueshiba (1883-1969). One the website of Aikido Australia (www.aikidoaus.com.au), Aikido is described in this way:

"It is based upon principles of non-aggression, non-resistance, and non-competitiveness, it is unique in that it allows people to defend themselves against larger and stronger attackers, without requiring great strength or speed, yet it also teaches us to understand and respect our fellow Man. The gentle quality of Aikido makes it appealing to men and women and children regardless of age. It not only offers spiritual development, mental concentration, balance, reflex action and exercise, but also teaches proper etiquette and behaviour."

Emotional Aikido follows similar principles of non-aggression, non-resistance, and non-competitiveness. Emotional Aikido is about being fully present to yourself as well as to the other person, so that energy can flow between you without causing harm.

The first principle of Emotional Aikido, as it is with the practical martial art, is deep self-awareness and strong personal control. In Emotional Aikido, we master ourselves first – physically and emotionally. Then we learn how to let emotional energy flow constructively.

Emotional Aikido principle 1: Master physicality

When it comes to interpersonal entanglements, it's physicality that matters first. Whether we like it or not, we are bags of bio-chemical soup. Our hormones and internal chemistry skew our responses to people, circumstances, and ideas. We experience this first as teenagers when our puberty hormones create all sorts of mayhem. As adults, we know how challenging it is to be optimistic, focused, and even pleasant when we are deprived of sleep, suffering from the 'hangries' (hungry and angry), or 'hormonal'.

Emotions are naturally occurring biochemical events. There is a direct correlation between what we consume and how we feel. In *High Life 24/7*, Matt Church asserts, "You can change your mood through your food." Emotional eaters like me know this to be true. A glass of red wine and a block of chocolate feels like compensation for a stressful day.

Some emotions are a result of imbalances too. Not enough serotonin in the body can result in depression, stress, and guilt. We can moderate hormones through use of nutrition, physical activity, exposure to sunlight, and sometimes medication.

Our key responsibility as centered leaders is to master our physical needs first. We need to take elevated self-care to ensure we are at our best physically, and thus mentally and emotionally as well. This means ensuring adequate rest, optimum nutrition and hydration, and vigorous exercise on most days. This helps us moderate our hormones and thus our moods.

Many world leaders are famous in their advocacy of physical fitness as a key aspect of their success in business, politics, entertainment, or religion. Among these are Dr Kiran Bedi, Sir Richard Branson, and US President Barack Obama.

World-class leadership needs world-class physical self-mastery.

Emotional Aikido principle 2: Master emotions

Sometimes it's physicality that drives emotional response. Other times it is conscious and unconscious thoughts that trigger emotional sensations. Let's take a deeper look at the thought-to-emotion relationship.

Emotions are essentially energy currency in the body. This is why emotions have sometimes been defined as 'energy in motion', or e-motion.

Emotions and the human volcano

Emotions drive behaviour. We perceive human behaviour the way we observe a volcano: sometimes dormant, sometimes explosive, sometimes just simmering, only observable from a distance, from the outside. Human behaviour bubbles up from the core of our inner volcano, from the raw material of human engagement and one's personal biochemical lava.

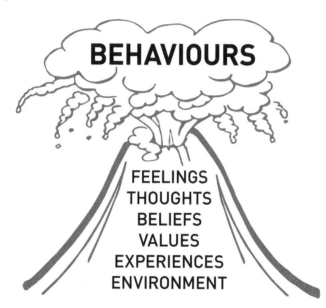

What happens on the inside? What causes the eruptions? The volcano funnels experiences, values, thoughts, and feelings into behaviour choices that erupt like the smoke from a volcano.

It all starts in our specific environments. This is the time and place of our birth and upbringing. A person who was born in rural China in the 1950s will have a very different upbringing and environment from a person who is born in 2015 in Sydney, Australia. Physical surroundings, family and social environment, and cultural norms all start to shape who we are, what we think, and what we value.

What we witness and experience in our surroundings helps us to form opinions on what we do and do not like. These likes and dislikes become our values. Values are what we cherish. They form the basis of all decisions.

With more life experience, we start to build rules around what we do and don't like – these become our beliefs. Beliefs are thoughts that we repeat over and over until we feel they are true. They are nothing more than habitual thought. However, this collection of beliefs forms our world view, how we choose to see and respond to the world.

Beliefs act like shortcuts for our brain to process new experiences, environments and people we meet. New experiences get filtered through the mental database held in the subconscious mind, much like data is filtered through software for processing. Based on what is held in the belief software, a response is issued to the conscious mind.

The response occurs first as a thought. This thought generates an electrical signal that we experience as a feeling. As thoughts are in various shades of positive or negative, this is how we experience various shades of emotions. Feelings are essentially sensations created in the body in response to thought.

Thoughts and their subsequent feelings will cause us to react, creating a behaviour. Positive thoughts generate a certain type of behaviour such as smiling, laughing, or friendly social engagement. Negative thoughts trigger other types of behaviour – anything from aggression to withdrawal.

These behaviours can create positive or negative outcomes in our lives.

Case study: Money doesn't grow on trees

A young boy grows up in industrial England, the son of a coal miner and schoolteacher. His parents work long hours for little pay. There is enough food to go around, and he attends a public school with other kids whose parents work at the mine, or in the local town. For this family there are no overseas trips and no brand new clothes every season. Clothes are passed down from siblings or bought at the local thrift shop, and toys are limited. The parents often fight about who is spending what, and how they are going to pay the various bills. The atmosphere is often tense. The boy's mother tells the boy and his two sisters: "Money doesn't grow on trees".

In this environment the boy subconsciously creates thought patterns around money: money causes stress, there is never enough money, money is given reluctantly, spending money on 'frivolous' things is a bad thing.

With these thought patterns about money, what happens to the boy as he grows up?

Thoughts of money evoke feelings of tension, stress, pressure, and bitterness. It becomes a love/hate relationship: he knows he needs money to engage in basic human social functions, but the getting of it is hard, laborious, and full of stress. The boy becomes a replica of his parents in his behaviour and his choices, and passes this environment, these values, and these beliefs down to his own children, thereby perpetuating the cycle of struggle.

So how could he break this cycle?

Let's say the boy gets to go on a school excursion one day. He meets some kids from another school in England and makes a new friend. The new friend invites him over to play. The new friend's parents are doctors. They are a lot wealthier than his parents and the friend's lifestyle is a lot more relaxed and abundant. All of the sudden, the boy has a new experience and a new environment to shape his world view. With continued exposure to this environment and experiences, the boy's thought patterns start to shift, and he develops the idea of new possibilities, new attitudes, and new behaviours.

Other people's volcanoes

What we see of others is what comes out of the top of the volcano – the behaviour. This is what we tend to react to and make judgements about.

Centered leaders learn to master their own volcanoes first. We create environments that support us emotionally, physically, mentally, and spiritually. We choose our values and assess our beliefs regularly, as discussed in the Renewal chapter. We make sure that our biochemical 'lava' is clean through regular sleep, good nutrition, and plenty of exercise. This way we minimise our own emotional volcanic explosions.

It also means that we are able to assess other people's volcanic explosions with compassion and curiosity, as opposed to judgement. We can wonder as we observe someone's behaviour, "what might be in their volcano to cause them to react that way?"

INSIGHT

If you don't ask, you don't know

On one of my canoe trips, my co-tripper Jo and I had an altercation over a pot of coffee. We were packing up camp, the wind was coming up, and it was a bit of a dreary day. Jo asked me to make the coffee. I was in the middle of stuffing my sleeping bag into its tiny bag. This was akin to shoving a kangaroo into a pillowcase and was my least favourite task. I snapped, "I'm in the middle of something right now, Jo."

"Fine. I'll do it myself." She grabbed the coffee pot, stormed down to the shore of the lake, and kept walking.

I thought this was a bit of an over-reaction, even with my moody reply being a little provocative. I sighed, prepared an apology and chased after her.

I'm glad I did. This moment was a turning point in our friendship for the trip. As I caught up with her, I apologised for being ill-tempered. She turned and blurted her concerns about the end of the trip. We had one week left out of six and it was all coming too quickly to an end. She felt we had not spent that much time together and she realised I would soon be heading off to Montreal for the year and she would miss me. We had had an incredible year together traveling around Mexico, and then this epic six-week canoe trip. I would miss her too.

We made up and made the most of the trip together, steadfast friends for life.

Sometimes it's a little tiff that erupts. Sometimes it's silence that may trigger an emotional cascade. I had a meeting with an enthusiastic prospective client and she agreed that she was ready to start an executive coaching program. I called her the next week to make arrangements. No answer. I left messages. I emailed. This went on for weeks.

I had a few choices: keep trying, wait and see, or give up. I also had a few internal narratives to explain this avoidance behaviour: she's ignoring me, she wants to cancel, she's sick and/ or injured.

I chose to give her the benefit of the doubt, and kept trying.

Then the response came in my inbox, "Sorry I haven't been in touch. As you know my father has been unwell and has taken a turn for the worse. As I am the primary caregiver, I've been a little pre-occupied. I'll get back to you when I can." We don't know what's in people's volcanoes. It serves us best as centered leaders to respond first with curiosity and compassion. This also helps keep us from getting carried away with our own internal dialogue and subsequent emotional eruptions.

Skills for mastering emotions

1. The 'feeling into feeling' exercise

As with any martial art, influence starts with the self. In Emotional Aikido, it is the same. Now that we have an understanding of where feelings come from, we can look at how to manage them.

The first thing to know is that *we do not need to suppress, ignore, or get rid of any feeling*, no matter how distasteful or even anti-social it may be. Feelings only become issues for us if we bottle them up, or if we give them free rein. We want neither! Remember – we're in charge. We have feelings, but they don't own us.

Since feelings are just energy in the body, we can *start our management of them by observing them*. This takes some self-awareness.

Notice when a feeling arises. Being able to then identify the feeling is one of the first key skills of emotional intelligence. Naming the emotion is the first step in getting some observational distance.

Next, we can take a deep dive with our imagination into that feeling. Focus on where it is in the body. Where is the most intense part of that feeling? Throat? Chest? Stomach? Head? Use your imagination to zero in on it.

Now use your imagination and observe your feelings:

- Shape
- Texture
- Colour
- Temperature

Imagine now you're a tiny space traveller. Imagine flying like a mini Superman into the feeling, to its very epicentre. Then just sit in the centre of the feeling, observing, as you breathe and let the feeling happen all around you.

Imagine stretching out in the feeling, making room around you. Observe any changes.

After a minute or so, imagine flying out through the bottom of the feeling out in to the fresh air again. Take a minute to observe your inner world, check your body, and open your eyes. Has the feeling-shape changed at all?

What we find in doing the 'feeling into feeling' exercise is that the feeling will shift, diminish or lessen. The simple act of paying deep attention to the energy in the body acts like pressure valve and releases some of the pent up energy. This allows the neocortex and our Higher Self voice to come back into action to deal with the situation at hand.

2. Pendulum practice

Another way to get some distance between yourself and your emotions is to do pendulum practice.

Imagine that emotions are like a pendulum that swings between two poles, negative and positive. If we are not conscious and mindful of our emotions, we can feel carried away by them, as if we were at the end of the pendulum and being swung between the two poles. Trying to stop the pendulum at one pole or the other only leads to a bigger swing.

It is better to imagine we are at the apex of the pendulum, observing the swing of emotions, allowing them, but not trying to resist or persist with either emotion. In this way we can experience emotions without getting attached to or pushed around by them. Emotions are going to happen regardless, so if we allow them to ebb and flow in a natural way, with conscious awareness, we can remain centered, engaged, and focused.

3. Reducing the pendulum's swing

There are three main strategies to reduce the volatility of emotions, or the pendulum swing:

1. Rigorous self-care, as explained previously in the Master physicality section.

2. Play traffic cop for your thoughts. Since thoughts generate emotional responses, pay attention first to your emotions and then to the thoughts that are causing them. Catch yourself in the middle of a thought, and check if it's positive or negative. If it's positive, let it through. If it's negative, re-direct it to something more positive and constructive.

My favourite re-orienting question that re-positions my emotional focus is this:

"What do I want instead?" This will always generate a positive focus.

3. Meditate. The break from a frenetic, busy mind is like a sip of water in the desert. Meditation, or disciplines like breathing concentration and yoga, are a great way of boosting the parasympathetic nervous system and calming the adrenals. When we calm our mind, the biology and emotions follow.

Emotional Aikido principle 3: Master inner voices

Emotions also occur as a result of our self-talk. We all talk to ourselves. Generally this is a constant stream of reactive drivel. We comment on the weather, we berate ourselves, we tell ourselves we are bored, frustrated, envious, scared. There is constant noise in our own heads, of our own making! These are all thoughts, and all thoughts have emotional responses, in various shades of positive or negative.

The Gremlin voice

Sigmund Freud wrote extensively about the ego, the id, and the superego. For our purposes, consider the ego as the personalised expression of the individual as a separate entity. It is the interface between self and other embodied spirits. It is the navigator of the material world, and helps us steer through the complex social realms of human interactions.

The ego has a very clear purpose: to ensure our individual survival. It is linked with the limbic system – the system that comprises the thalamus (processing sensory messages) and the amygdala (which triggers emotional responses). If there is a perceived threat or emergency, the amygdala can hijack the brain and override the more rational, logical side of the neocortex: the 'fight or flight' response.

The ego may have several voices. These are not psychic delusions or multiple personalities, but aspects of ourselves that give different perspectives.

Such voices may include the critic, the worry-wart, the editor, the victim, the threat-perceiver, the catastrophiser and so on. I call this voice the Gremlin!

The Gremlin voice is:

- Noisy
- Reactive
- Demanding
- Argumentative
- Over-active.

The Gremlin also helps us to interact with others and focuses on keeping us safe. As such, the Gremlin:

- Is concerned with self, individual, and personal concerns
- Feels separate and disconnected
- Feels like it is 'me' against the world
- Sees problems everywhere
- Is easily triggered to fight or flight

- Tries to gain control over fears with power, pleasing others, perfectionism, addictions
- Sees scarcity everywhere, is grasping, and never satisfied
- Wants to be right all the time
- Is about separation, isolation, self-protection, scarcity, short-term thinking, win/lose
- Tends to tune into all the problems in life and tunes out all the little daily joys.

The Gremlin voice is an unpleasant and volatile master if we let it have court over our thinking and feeling processes. Working in conjunction with our Higher Self voice, however, the Gremlin voice becomes a useful servant.

The Higher Self voice

This is a quieter voice, a deeper voice. This is the voice from our Higher Selves, or our inner wisdom.

How do we have two voices? We can turn to brain science for some help. The brain has been mapped to show various functions critical to survival, as well as for social interactions and higher reflection. The Higher Self is often associated with the neocortex – the most recent evolution of the rational mind associated with complex thought. The Higher Self voice is a part of ourselves that is connected to a deeper, wiser, place. It is often the quietest voice as we begin our spiritual and self-awareness journey.

The Higher Self is the part of us that is unselfish, loving, wise, eternal, peaceful and deep joy. It is the expression of wisdom and compassion, the best of the heart and the best of the mind. It is the part of us that seeks unity with others, the Universe, God or Higher Power.

The Higher Self voice is:

- Focused on unity, connection, service, abundance, long-term thinking, win/win solutions
- Tuned into all the little joys of life while not flinching from problems.

If we leverage the altruistic and connected aspects of the Higher Self Voice in partnership with the survival-oriented ego voice, then we start to have a balance of wisdom and compassion. This looks like concern for humanity while balanced with concern for self. They are not mutually exclusive.

How do inner voices affect our emotions?

These two voices, the Higher Self and the Gremlin, trigger emotional responses. These either serve us well, or distract us and drive us to unhelpful and sometimes destructive behaviours.

Emotions serve as feedback from your Higher Self as to whether what we are thinking and doing is in alignment with your Higher Path.

Emotions are our inner guidance

- If it feels *good*, then the situation, thought, action is serving us well.
- If it feels *bad*, then the situation, thought, action is not serving us.

This is the start of developing our inner voices, our intuition, our 'spider sense'.

INSIGHT

Accessing my inner voice in a crisis

I was waiting at the finish line of the Fun Run on an overcast day, shivering while I waited for my husband, Rob. Just in front of me one of the runners pulled up short, and careened to the side to fall on his back. Runners around him leaped out of the way, and one or two stepped on him by accident. The fallen man didn't flinch. I glanced around and saw no one was coming to his aid.

"Ok, I guess it's up to me."

Twenty years of First Aid training kicked in as I crouched down beside the man. I leaned over him, looking in to his face. "Hi, my name is Zoë – can you hear me?"

The man stared back at me with wide, unresponsive eyes. It was like looking at eye-shaped glass bulbs.

I squeezed his shoulder and again, no response. I sat back on my heels as I studied him. This was not like First Aid training. When your training partner pretended to be unresponsive there was some sign of movement, however small. With this man, nothing.

A quiet, calm voice spoke inside my head. "I guess we had better roll him." Of course. If you have a breathing, non-responsive patient, you roll them to the side to monitor and keep the airway open. So I scooped him up and rolled him over, being mindful to ease his head onto his arm. He was light as a rag doll. Someone ran over to check his carotid. I knew he had a pulse, as I could see him breathing. They ran away again. Off to my right a woman appeared in my peripheral view. I heard her cry, "That's my husband!" She dashed away.

I was alone in a sea of hundreds as they streamed past us in the frenzy and excitement of a Fun Run finish line.

"Speak to him," the voice in my head said. Of course, reassure the patient. "I know First Aid. Someone's on their way. We've sent for help." I kept my hands on his shoulders and leaned over him to check his breathing. Still good.

The St John Ambulance officers arrived and they gave him oxygen. It started to rain, so I opened up the umbrella and held it over the young man and the attendant. The grass was so green, and so quiet, even as the throng of a hundred people swirled around us.

People arrived with a tarp and pulled it over the trio. "Go to his wife," said the voice. I knew she must be nearby, and she was, with a 10-year-old boy and a little girl in a pram. I introduced myself and put my arm around the woman who was shivering. Her son asked, "What's happening to Dad?"

The St John Ambulance officers arrived and they gave him oxygen. It started to rain, so I opened up the umbrella and held it over the young man and the attendant. The grass was so green, and so quiet, even as the throng of a hundred people swirled around us.

People arrived with a tarp and pulled it over the trio. "Go to his wife," said the voice. I knew she must be nearby, and she was, with a 10-year-old boy and a little girl in a pram. I introduced myself and put my arm around the woman who was shivering. Her son asked, "What's happening to Dad?"

She said, "Dad's had a bit of trouble and they're helping him."

"What are they doing to him?"

They had rolled the young man on his back. I could see his legs underneath the tarp, and his abdomen heaving.

"They're helping him to breathe, honey."

They had started cardiopulmonary resuscitation and they were helping his heart to beat. I didn't know that when you administered CPR that the abdomen jumped up and down as if breathing from heavy exercise. I could feel the woman's heart beating against her rib cage like a frightened sparrow.

I don't know how long this went on. It could have been thirty minutes; it could have been two. I remember the gentle patter of rain on the umbrella, the warmth of my arm around the woman, and the noise of the crowd like a bubbling soundtrack.

The attendants bundled the young man into the ambulance, and one of them came to speak to us. They were taking him to hospital, and his wife was to follow with the children.

I found out later that the young man's name was Geoff. Just 28, and he didn't make it. Something in his heart had burst. I realised then that I was likely the last person he saw alive.

It wasn't the first time I'd heard the voice that guided me through this experience. It had appeared in far more mundane times, like driving or in the shower. And then it spoke with ideas for business, or observations on the traffic. I'd always thought it was me talking to myself. Me, but with a non-male and non-female voice. Perhaps it was. I just know that I was grateful on that day for the deep, stoic calm with which it guided me to help this young man and his family.

I know now that with repeated meditation and guided visualisation, this kind of clarity and focus is available at times other than crisis. I can access this deeper wisdom at any time, as long as I sink into that relaxed state on a regular basis. How wonderful it is to have that deep all-knowing reassurance and advice on tap.

Emotional Aikido principle 4: Master the flow of energy from others

Mirror neurons[5] in the brain can also spark emotions. These mirror neutrons replicate what they observe in others, sending us clues as to how others are feeling so we 'catch' their emotion. This is how emotion can be contagious. Incidentally, a good mood is more contagious than a bad mood.

The exception is when it's the leader's mood. The leader's mood is broadcast like a megaphone. This is because historically we are tuned to the leader as the 'protector' of the group. If the leader was relaxed, we knew we were safe. If they were anxious, we knew there was trouble brewing.

This is how we feel other people's feelings. It's the origins of empathy and compassion. This can be useful to build rapport and understanding. Sometimes other people's emotions can be so intense, however, that they cause our own pendulum to swing and we find ourselves being pushed unwittingly around by emotion.

INSIGHT

When emotional entanglement dances with your emotional energy

When we engage with others, emotions can run high. If we are not centered, we can get knocked off our perch as a result.

In one conversation with a client, let's call him Neil, he described the conversation with the managing partner of his firm.

---

5 See Daniel Goleman, *Social Intelligence: The New Science of Human Relationships*, pp.68-72

Neil was under big pressure, as his team was not performing against budget. As a result, Neil was getting squeezed out of the partnership, excluded from strategic meetings, and had his drawings cut by twenty per cent. Normally a very stoic man, Neil was wide-eyed, with a red flush on his throat. As he described in detail the dastardly political manoeuvrings of his colleagues and the unfair and underhanded backroom deals, I felt myself getting pulled in to the story.

When our meeting finished, Neil left with a counter-negotiation plan. I was left reeling. For the first time in 12 years of executive coaching, I realised I'd been soaking up his energy. I did not think to enact Emotional Aikido strategies because Neil presented as outwardly calm. Upset, but calm.

My body told me otherwise. I felt sick to my stomach. I never usually react to client issues, as my role is to be the calm and centered supporter, to help them work their way through the issues. On this occasion, I was knocked for six by the invisible yet volatile emotional energy of the situation.

Once I acknowledged what was going on, I did the 'feel into the feeling' exercise and the nausea and tension subsided.

There are ways of avoiding this kind of emotional entanglement. These are essential skills for any leader as we are often in high-pressure conversations where the stakes are high and emotions run hot.

Five Emotional Aikido skills to calm the emotions when with others:

1. *Intention:* Remember the purpose of the engagement. This will help settle nerves and bring the big picture back into focus. This can be the anchor in tense exchanges, bringing both parties back to the point of the exchange.

2. *Awareness:* Maintain awareness of self and other, and what energy is emerging. If I had been more mindful with Neil, I would have noticed his signs of agitation and been more careful in protecting myself from their impact.

3. *Connection:* I use a visualisation technique to connect me to Higher Self consciousness. This in turn helps protect me from other people's energy. It's the shape of the octahedron: two pyramids with their bases pressed together. Imagine the top of one pyramid is above the head and the tip of the other below the feet, like a giant diamond around the body. Ask all unhelpful energy to leave and be transmuted into good energy, and call back all personal energy dispersed in the universe. Then imagine the octahedron filling with white light, streaming down from the sun through the top of the octahedron. This is my basic connection and protection visualisation, and it is absolutely amazing how helpful it is.

4. *Diversion:* This is an actual physical move. When sitting or standing with someone who is experiencing high levels of emotional energy, simply shift aside and open up the angle between you. This allows the emotional energy broadcasting from them to sail straight past. This way we can still be fully present to the other person, while not absorbing or getting caught up in their story. If I had done this with Neil I would have avoided the intense side effects of his emotional wake.

5. *Connect with soul:* When we pay attention and deeply appreciate someone for the spirit-made-flesh entity that they are, then the deep ocean of compassion swallows them, and us, in its embrace. Compassion is the highest form of love. It's the expression of deep appreciation with a desire to help and make a difference if you can. It's the message of, "I see you, I know you, and I appreciate you as a fellow human traveller with a world of woes, worries, and dreams, trying to do your best, even if it looks completely whacked from the outside."

That kind of complete acceptance is a warm woolly embrace that allows conversations to go from noise to meaning.

What's the effect of Emotional Aikido?

When we match our intention with complete attention, we send the message: *"You are important"*.

When we match our attention with an attitude of appreciating soul, we send the message: *"You are heard"*.

When we match our attitude of soul appreciation with an open body position, we send the message: *"You are safe."*

INSIGHT

Caving with the octahedron

I used the octahedron exercise when I was caving with a group on a leadership development program. They were tasked with a search-and-rescue mission, and they were behind schedule. Anxiety was running high, and individuals were making rash decisions, putting themselves at risk in an awkward environment. I noticed that I started to get anxious too. I was looking around for my colleague who was due to meet us deep in the cave. He was nowhere to be seen, and I started to feel the flutter of nerves.

Then I caught myself. I realised I was soaking up the energy of the group. I had nothing to be worried about. I knew my colleague was fine. He was a masterful and experienced caver and he was near to the exit and our support team. I was fine too. I was an experienced caver and the environment was controlled, with good access, and I was no more than five minutes from the exit. I could see all the group members, and though they appeared to be a bit frenetic, they were not in danger to themselves or me.

I imagined the octahedron around me, and focused on letting their energy go. I could then sit and observe the dynamics of the group process and let it be tense. This was after all one of the more important activities for the group! How they dealt with the pressure would be key to their breakthrough as a team.

Their tension and anxiety swirled around me, and I sat safely in my octahedron, observing, and waiting. Eventually they erupted in conflict and a decision was made. In the debrief, their experience as a group working through that anxiety and stress was a significant peak learning experience. Had I not done the octahedron exercise, very likely my own stress would have risen, and I might have interceded too early, ruining the learning experience for the group.

Emotional Aikido is really about allowing our emotions to flow in service to our journey, instead of against it. Emotions are after all what makes life so juicy! The highs of happiness exist only in contrast to the depths of sadness. We want to experience all of our emotions. We just don't want to be ruled by them. Likewise we want to accept people and their emotional responses rather than judge them. When we learn to dance and disarm emotion, it gives us the ability to connect more deeply with ourselves, and then with others.

Key points for connection

Emotional Aikido principle 1: Master physicality

Upgrade your physical, emotional, mental, and spiritual self-care.

Emotional Aikido principle 2: Master emotions

- Feel into the core of the feelings
- Pendulum practice
- Reduce pendulum swing: physical self-mastery, meditation, thought traffic cop.

Emotional Aikido principle 3: Master inner voices

Listen and pay attention to the voices within. Learn to identify the Gremlin voice and the Higher Self voice. Use them both to serve higher engagement with others as well as for self-mastery.

Emotional Aikido principle 4: Master the flow of energy from others

- **Intention:** why are you having the conversation? What is the ultimate objective?
- **Awareness:** what energy is emerging in the conversation?
- **Connection:** use the octahedron shape to connect with Higher Self and deflect other people's energies
- **Diversion:** move out of the way of other people's emotional expression
- **Connect with soul:** accept completely the other person as another living soul.

The Road Home, Or The Road Out Again

Our journeys are cyclical. We explore, we are challenged, we fail and falter and succeed, and hopefully, we learn. Whatever we learn, we can take with us, or teach to others. At this point in the journey we need time to reflect and process our experiences, make sense of them, and take what's useful from them. It's a time to reflect and recharge.

The Hindu Gods Shiva and Shakti provide a useful way to represent this process. They are the essence of creation and destruction for the purpose of growth and renewal.

I first learned of Shiva and Shakti when I was 16 and went to India with my friend Shilpa and her family, Indians who had migrated to Canada. It was 1986, and India was a waking giant. Looking back now, I think of how the young naïve Crusaders might have felt on their way to the Holy Land. Focused on their 'mission', then confronted with the dazzling beauty and wonders of the East. They no doubt experienced this clash of worldviews as a shock, to which they responded by trying to subdue others to their own will.

Learning can be like the Crusaders' experience: shock at a new paradigm, and wanting to reject and subdue it to protect our own version of the truth.

If we're open to other experiences, however, it can be enlightening instead of shocking. India, for example, I experienced as a cacophony of sound, colour, tastes, and humanity. Everything was new and amazing to me, seen through my young eyes. I marvelled at the food, at the families who lived together with aunts, uncles, parents, together with servants. Just outside, the ladies in their faded saris swept the fields with bunches of twigs.

It was here I started to learn of Hindu spirituality. We went to many temples and Shilpa's mother patiently told me of their numerous Gods. They had a shrine at home and would pray to it daily. For a young girl raised without a religion or spiritual practice, this was fascinating and mysterious.

On subsequent trips to India I have wondered at the collective surge of development – mad, wild, chaotic, yet deeply spiritual. I watched one Tuesday night as young barefoot devotees dressed in modern casual pants and western-style tops, lined up outside of a temple to pay their respects and say their prayers.

The Hindu concept of time as cyclical baffled me the most. In the Hindu cosmos, the world is created, then after millennia destroyed, only to be created anew. This story sounded familiar, and the Biblical flood stories of Noah and the Ark came to mind. But time as cyclical? Surely it marches on, unfolding one day after another?

Yet everything is cyclical, in a pattern of death, destruction, and creation.

Nature is our greatest teacher in this regard. Leaves grow and nourish the tree, are shed in winter, fall to the ground, decompose and nourish the tree once more. Walk in any forest and we can see death and new life at every turn.

When I learned of Shiva and Shakti, I found it a useful way to think and live into my renewal practices as a leader. Everything has a beginning and ending, and we can guide those forces deliberately to our advantage and to our purpose in service to the world.

Renewal is a process of letting go of what is no longer needed, resolving our deepest challenges, and growing into a new version of ourselves. We need the twin forces of creation and destruction in our lives if we are to expand and evolve. Like a snake sheds its skin, we need to slough off the old bits no longer needed, and grow into new skin, bigger and brighter.

Shiva and Shakti

In Hinduism, Shiva is one of the main Gods. He is seen as transcendent, formless, and unchanging. And yet he is also the creator and destroyer. He does not exist without his cosmic spouse, Shakti, who represents universal creative energy.

Shiva can be understood as consciousness, and Shakti as creative energy. Shiva as force, and Shakti as energy. Together they bring everything into the manifested world.

Shiva, known both as creator and destroyer, is understood to bring about destruction, to allow for new creation. He clears the path so something new may emerge. This is how Shiva and Shakti work together. Consciousness and creativity, destruction and creation.

For the centered leader, this principle is central to our practice of renewal. We need both consciousness and creativity, destruction and creation. We access the forces with planned renewal activity.

Renewal can be practiced on a daily basis as well as at planned intervals. My mentor Matt Church works on 10-week cycles: he plans a cycle of intense activity followed by a 2-week break. This way he can maintain focus and an intense pace knowing that a 2-week renewal phase is not far away.

My work cycle follows seasons too: I plan my holidays first – skiing in Australia's winter in August, skiing overseas in January, with some beach time in April. I also map out some couch time regularly throughout the month, especially after a busy period of travel and program delivery.

From a practical point of view the active component of my work looks like: travel, corporate facilitation, training delivery, outdoor programs, meeting swathes of clients and prospective clients, networking, connecting, writing, creating.

Over five parts, the renewal phase will look like this:

1. **Review:** Check in with alignment against vision, values, projects and decisions. This is how to check our integrity, and assess how we followed through on the promises we set for ourselves. It's a time to reflect and to acknowledge and celebrate successes as well.

2. **Reconnect:** Connect to guidance for any clarification, or for a boost of faith. We can do this with internal and external approaches, and from metaphysical to material aspects of guidance. Examples include journaling, card reading, meditating, and talking with mentors.

3. **Reinvent:** This is the vigorous interrogation of our internal dialogue. If our behaviour is not matching our expectations, overhaul our storytelling, reframe the experience, and reach for new affirmations and beliefs that are more supportive.

4. **Resolve:** This is tough work. It's delving into shadow and exploring what needs to be healed and resolved so we can be more integrated, peaceful and aligned with our purpose. It can be a bit yucky. Courage required!

5. **Refresh:** This follows the universal law of detachment as espoused by the Dalai Lama and many other religious faiths. This is about dropping attachment to outcomes, to challenges, even to life itself and being fully present, absorbed in the moment, savouring the sweetness of life.

1. Review

Schedule the reviews

There are three major time periods where we can sit down for a stocktake: end of the calendar year, end of our personal year (birthday), and at the end of each quarter. We may also add in another review at the end of an intense period of activity. I find this helps rekindle energy and passion. Weekly and daily reviews happen in conjunction with the planning process.

Quarterly reviews

There are two aspects to consider in our reviews: process and results. With process, ask:

- How much have I enjoyed this quarter?
- How do I feel about my experience?
- Did I behave the way I intended?
- Do I feel satisfied or unsatisfied with my results?
- What did I learn?
- Did I follow my plan? Why or why not?

Journal the answers.

With performance results, these questions are largely outcome-focused:

- Did I reach my goals? Why or why not?
- Who did I help?
- How much progress did I make towards my goals? What worked, what didn't?

Calendar year and personal year reviews

Here are some reflection questions for these reviews:

- How much of my theme is being expressed through me so far?
- Am I spending time with the people I said I wanted to?
- If I passed away tomorrow would I feel satisfied with my choices and how I focused my energy? Why or why not?
- What needs to change?
- What do I need to stop doing?
- What do I need to start doing?
- What support do I need?

Weekly reviews

At the end of each week, we assess how well we executed the plan. These more regular reviews are about focusing more on tactics than strategy. They also ensure there is progress towards our major goals.

Ask:

- Did I complete my mission critical tasks? Why or why not?
- What was great about this week?

- What were the sticking points, if any?
- What is being carried over to next week?

Daily reviews

At the end of each day, it's important to record successes – both process and outcomes, as well as do an attitude and focus check.

Ask:

- When was I on or off track today? Why?
- What were the three things that went well today?
- What are my wins/successes/achievements – either in terms of process or in outcomes?
- What questions or challenges do I have that I need to resolve or work through?
- How was my personal energy and my sense of enjoyment today?

With these questions answered and journaled, it's time for renewal through connection to source and inspiration.

2. Reconnect

In this phase of renewal, we move away from rational review to spiritual consultation. Logical pros and cons limit perspective and possibilities. If we expand our capacity for guidance through intuition, we can make better decisions.

As Albert Einstein said: "The intuitive mind is a sacred gift and the rational mind is a faithful servant. We have created a society that honours the servant and has forgotten the gift."

How do we bring back honouring our intuitive gift?

Without the full spectrum of guidance, it's like looking at a painting through a telescope: we miss the big picture. Adding guidance to our leadership process is like adding colours to our palette. Instead of seeing just in green, we see in rainbows.

Leaders with presence know they are not the font of all knowledge, that they are not in this game alone, and that it takes a team to make a champion.

So how and what and where does a leader with presence get guidance?

There are two domains to tap for support as leader: Mystical and Practical.

Mystical sources of guidance pre-suppose the leader has evolved to the point where they no longer rely solely on a concrete, evidence-based world, but that they are aware of forces that exist beyond the senses, and that they have tapped into the deep mystery of human existence.

This need not be a grandiose experience of revelation or enlightenment; simple observation of the forces of nature will open questions to the great mystery. Sit and observe a plant. Wonder at how it transforms the bare essentials of water, minerals, dirt, and sunshine into green foliage. We will find everyday miracles in a leaf and the beauty of a flower a true revelation.

Pondering the effortless coordination and integration of the natural world will humble even the most scientific of mind. How does it all work so seamlessly, this constant cycle of destruction and creation?

Mystical sources of guidance aim to access some of these realms of mystery.

Practical sources of guidance are more familiar and less esoteric. The two sources of practical guidance are advice and interpretation.

1. Advice

External, practical guidance is more familiar. These are the common areas we tend to go to for advice:

- Friend
- Peer
- Coach
- Mentor
- Community of practice*
- Mastermind**

*A *community of practice* is an association of professionals or colleagues who gather together around a particular topic or interest. In meetings, they share their own best practice, resources, and ideas to commonly experienced challenges. It is essentially a pooling of knowledge for the common benefit of all.

**A *mastermind* is a small group of peers, often in different professional areas of interests or different businesses. The mastermind acts like a board of advisors for each individual.

Getting good advice is like being a smart traveller. When we ask for tips on the best places to visit, what to avoid, yummy restaurants and so on, it saves us time, energy, and disappointment.

The value of good advice cannot be underestimated. It can increase revenue and it can transform lives.

When I joined Thought Leaders Business School, the first round of practical advice on how to structure my approach to business, and how to meet clients, saw my business income triple within three months. Not to mention saved me a mountain of lonely angst, wondering if I was on the right track.

INSIGHT

Wilderness advice

As a 17-year-old, I remember working at summer camp as a counsellor. My mentor, Brent Cuthbertson, was in charge of the Wilderness Canoe Tripping Program. He was what we called a 'Trail Legend', an experienced canoe trip leader who was leading one of the prestigious 6-week canoe trips. So when we were at a camp party and I found myself in conversation with him, I listened intently while trying to tone down my star-struck gaze.

He asked me what I wanted to do at camp down the track. I, of course, had not thought further than that summer. I was 17, and that was the sum of my big plans. Finishing high school. Pondering the opportunities of university.

He asked me, "Do you like Trail?" The canoe tripping program was referred to as the 'Trail' program. Being 'on Trail' was akin to utopia as far as I was concerned. I could think of nothing better than being on a canoe expedition in the wilderness of Canada.

"I LOVE Trail!" I gushed. "I would love to be back out there again." I had completed my own 6-week canoe trip the summer before, as a participant. It had been the single most significant thing in my life to date.

Brent said, "You could do this job. You could be the Wilderness Coordinator one day."

I balked. To be placed in his mind on equal footing as a Trail Legend! My eyes popped and my brain did a little hiccup seizure.

I let that one go.

It did, however, sink through the layers of my subconscious and grow as a seed of possibility. Could I? Did I want to? Was I ever going to be up to it?

A few years later, I found myself donning the mantle as leader of the Trail staff.

I had never really forgotten Brent's words. They had just percolated, growing from possibility to certainty. Such is the power of external advice: it can show us possible futures we may not dare to dream ourselves.

2. Interpretation

Using interpretation techniques provides us with a map and an index to explain the stories in our lives. It's another way of getting advice.

We are meaning-making creatures. We make meaning and stories about what happens to us, and why. Not all stories are empowering. We need to choose the ones that uplift and serve us well. There are great number of stories or 'patterns of meaning' that can serve as a map for our experiences.

Joseph Campbell's Hero's Journey is an example of a map that can help frame our experiences in a meaningful way. We might be undertaking challenges, striving towards apotheosis, or returning to teach others.

Any psychometric assessment tool such as Myers-Briggs, DiSC, Leadership Maturity Framework, or Enneagram, is a way of seeing patterns in our own behaviour, and that of others. It helps to provide a reference framework so we can navigate our way through experiences with some sort of focus and sense of awareness.

Guidance cards: One of my favourite tools for interpretation, more on the mystical scale, is using guidance cards. These come in enormous varieties such as Doreen Virtue's Goddess Cards, Osho Zen Tarot, or Abraham Hicks Abundance cards.

I use these cards as an opportunity for contemplation, rather than any sort of divining function. Because they are often archetypal in nature, it also helps for me to contemplate the gifts and challenges of the archetype, and where these elements may be playing out in my life.

The 'totality' Osho Zen Tarot card, for example, is an image of three trapeze artists – one swinging and releasing their companion to the third. Perfect timing and focus is required to execute this move.

Osho Zen Tarot explains: "In a trapeze act, nobody can afford to be a little bit absent, even for a split second. And it is this quality of total attentiveness to the moment at hand that is represented here. We may feel there are too many things to do at once, but get bogged down trying to do a bit here, a bit there, instead of taking one task at a time and getting on with it … Developing the knack of being total in responding to whatever comes, as it comes, is one of the greatest gifts you can give yourself. Taking one step through life at a time, giving each step your complete attention and energy, can bring a wondrous new vitality and creativity to all that you do." (pp.86-87)

INSIGHT

Therapists and energy workers

When I went through my cancer treatment, I had some 'interesting' experiences.

Just before my surgery, I had a strong feeling that my two grandmothers, both deceased, were in the room watching from a corner. They were looking after me as doctors injected the anaesthetic. I've always wondered if I imagined it or if it actually happened. In the end it does not matter, because I gained comfort from the thought of them being there, real or not.

Through my treatment I also sought alternative therapies to support my healing. I consulted a nutritionist, a Reiki therapist, and a cranial sacral therapist. The latter, Jason, has since become what I affectionately call my 'spiritual advisor dude'.

His energy work involved putting hands on my abdomen and channelling energy. I don't know how it really works, but at the time I felt something was better than nothing, and I was going to throw everything at my healing whether I understood it or not.

Jason had his hands on my abdomen for what seemed like forever. At one point I opened my eyes and there he was in the corner of the room, rifling through something on his bookshelf. But I thought his hands were on my abdomen. They felt 100 per cent like they were on my abdomen. Except they weren't.

It was one of the weirdest things that had happened to me. It upended my understanding of the material world and challenged what I thought I knew of experience; if you smelled it, felt it, saw it, was it there?

I started to research other ways of knowing and experiencing the world, including light workers and clairvoyants. Ten years on, I still can't explain what happened. I concluded that guidance can take all sorts of forms. So why not be open to messages and interpretation, whomever and however they come from? It is up to us after all to make meaning from what happens to us.

Composure

There is a well-known adage that says 'it's not what happens to us that matters, but what we think about what happens to us.' This is empowering because it opens up experiences and adventures rather than shutting them down. That's why I'll take the opportunity to get a tarot reading, or see a psychic, or a clairvoyant. It's like opening the door to a whole new territory of adventure and discovery!

Use your experiences as opportunities for reflection and contemplation; to filter, digest, and then use what's helpful on the journey.

3. Intuition

Intuition moves us towards the more mystical aspects of guidance. Sometimes it's best to lean on our own internal advice and trust our intuition. Intuition is our internal compass that tells us when we are on or off course.

Our internal guidance system, our intuition, is simply our feelings. Our feelings take up residence and speak to us through our body. When we listen carefully, the body will tell us whether or not we are making choices that support our higher interests or not.

Daniel Goleman explains where intuition comes from biologically and neurologically. He says:

*"**You need to depend on your body's signals.** Monitoring of our internal organs is done by the insula, tucked behind the frontal lobes of the brain. The insula maps our body's insides via circuitry linking to our gut, heart, liver, lungs—every organ has its specific spot. This lets the insula act as a control center for organ functions, sending signals to the heart to slow its beat, the lungs to take a deeper breath… The insula attunes us to more than just our organs; our very sense of how we are feeling depends on it… Our 'gut feelings' are messages from the insula and other bottom-up circuits that simplify life decisions for us by guiding our attention toward smarter options. The better we are at reading these messages, the better our intuition… The 'Somatic marker' is neuroscientist Antonio Damasio's term for the sensation in our body that tells us when a choice feels wrong or right. This bottom-up circuitry telegraphs its conclusions through our gut feelings, often long before the top-down circuits come to a more reasoned conclusion.*

The ventromedial prefrontal area, a key part of this circuitry, guides our decision making when we face life's most complex decisions, like who to marry or whether to buy a house. Such choices can't be made by a cold, rational analysis. Instead we do better to simulate what it would feel like to choose A versus B. This brain area operates as that inner rudder.[6]

What Goleman and Damasio are saying is that the body is a finely-tuned sensory processing instrument that can tap much more information than the rational brain alone. Our body sensations, our gut feelings – our intuition – can provide us with deep, rich guidance.

Honouring our intuition takes practice. It needs development of internal awareness. It means harnessing the ability to feel things fully, to embrace emotions and allow them to be expressed and processed within a safe environment.

Learning to identify feelings first of all can be the first hurdle for many. In a logic-biased and task-biased culture, checking on feelings has been derided as effeminate and touchy-feely. Bringing feelings back to the leadership conversation creates a full spectrum conversation and perspective.

It begins by paying attention to the body. Doing an internal body scan each morning and checking, "how do I feel this morning?" is an important practice to develop an internal tuning in. Developing subtleties on emotional self-awareness will also allow greater expression of emotions.

We are taught not to express our emotions because we are afraid they will erupt inappropriately, or that we will be seen as weak or out of control. Suppression of emotion only leads to greater pressure, and so explosive emotional vomit results.

Consider instead the possibility of being able to communicate how you're feeling with compassion towards yourself, without doing an emotional spray over your listener. This shows poise, self-mastery, and open-hearted vulnerability and strength.

---

6 http://www.danielgoleman.info/daniel-goleman-how-to-hear-your-inner-voice-2/

How intuition relates to being a centered leader: In *Thought Leadership – Moving Hearts and Minds* by Robin Ryde, he cites the ability to include questions on feelings as a key component to strategic thinking. Being guided by feelings, as well as rational thought, is a key component of the centered leader. The centered leader has feelings; they are just not befuddled by them.

The centered leader knows they are human, and they give themselves permission to feel. They also know that by paying attention, by tuning their awareness into their feelings, they can dissipate the tension and friction that some negative feelings can cause, as we saw in the Connection chapter on Emotional Aikido.

Our emotional guidance system will always point us in one right direction, the direction that serves our soul and higher purpose. So often we override it because of the stories we've built up around ourselves about what we *must* do, out of obligation or duty. The truth is, we always have a choice. We can live our lives on our own terms.

A centered leader knows what those terms are, and balances their emotional response by following their inner compass.

4. Inspiration

Inspiration is also in the realm of the mystical. Inspiration is an inhalation: of new ideas, of new possibilities. We have infinite access to inspiration, when we pay attention. New ideas emerge from the unique connections of our inner world. All things in the world were ideas first. For example, legend has it that Paul McCartney composed the melody for *Yesterday* from a dream he had one night in 1964.

Going into a relaxed, detached state of awareness is one way to access inspiration. This is one of the reasons that meditation is so timelessly encouraged for boosting the parasympathetic nervous system (the rest and digest system) while calming the sympathetic nervous system (the fight and flight system).

Prayer can also serve this function. It is a process of focused concentration, asking specifically for inspiration, protection, and guidance.

Dreams are also a rich source of inspiration. They are the processing by-product of the subconscious mind, and offer plenty of opportunity for reflection and insight. My favourite dream interpretation strategy is outlined by Martha Beck in her book, *Steering by Starlight*.

Journaling is an excellent way to allow our own inner voice to shine through. Having a conversation with oneself through journal writing also serves to purge worries, concerns, and unhelpful thoughts.

In Deepak Chopra's fabulous book, *Synchrodestiny*, he encourages us to take note of the small synchronicities that occur in daily life. The person who emails as we are thinking of them, the book that jumps off the bookshelf as we are pondering an issue, the article that arrives in our inbox that is just what we needed for inspiration and decision-making. Deepak would say this is the Universal Consciousness speaking its whispered message of support and guidance. This is our soul speaking.

We can use signs and synchronicities to find powerful, positive frames for our experiences.

For example, I choose to believe that everything that happens to me is in my best interest, even if I can't see how in the moment. What this means on a day-to-day basis is when a client cancels an appointment, I accept this is in my best interest and something good will come of it, for me and my client. Or when a program is cancelled, I take this as encouragement from the universe that something bigger, better, and more in line with my vision and purpose is coming my way.

3. Reinvent beliefs

Advice, interpretation, intuition, and inspiration gives us good fodder for what's next in our quest. Before we surge ahead, we also need to check to see if our beliefs are supporting us or not. We need to reflect on what's working and not working in our lives and work. Quite often we'll find that a lot of what is not working, if at all, is due to faulty belief software. 'Software' is the pattern of beliefs we have installed through our experiences and environment that help us to make decisions on a daily basis, often subconsciously.

Beliefs are simple thoughts that we have repeated over and over until we feel they are true. Often they are arbitrary and have evolved out of conditioning, social circumstances, upbringing, reading, and other inputs. A common example is 'money is the root of all evil'. If this phrase is adopted as a 'truth' (a thought becomes a truth when it is repeated often enough), it becomes part of our belief software. What happens is that whenever the topic of money emerges in our life, it triggers the 'money is the root of all evil' belief software, and initiates behaviour that supports that belief. In this case, if we feel that money is the root of all evil, it must also be evil, and then we assiduously avoid money since we also want to avoid things that are 'evil'.

This can create problems for us if we also want to use money for purchasing or functioning in the world. We end up avoiding the thing that would aid us to achieve some of our goals. As centered leaders however, we need to be extraordinarily mindful of how our belief system is operating, the common beliefs we hold, and how they are serving us.

Beliefs drive all behaviour. So if beliefs are left unexamined and are not chosen deliberately, we are living in reaction to our environment and circumstances and not deliberately at all. The starting point for reflection on our beliefs is just that point where we ask: 'how is our life right now, is it good news or bad news?'

Belief Buster Matrix

	Internal	External (left brain)	Imagine (right brain)
Stage 1: Review	**1. DIAGNOSE** What is wrong?	**2. APPRECIATE** What is right?	**3. RE-ORIENT** What do I want instead?
Stage 2: Upgrade	**4. MANTRA** "I am"	**5. MEASURE** How will I know? Look for evidence	**6. MEME** Create story of future self
Stage 3: Reinforce	**7. REHEARSE** What if... How does x do y? Read/feel the story	**8. TRACK** Success journal	**9. ANCHOR** Pimp my environment

Here is the entire process I use, called the Belief Buster Matrix, on how to review and then reinvent our beliefs, and thus our choices, and our very lives. A detailed explanation is given in the table on the next page.

Stage one: Review

Step 1. Diagnose

As a species we are often more motivated to change by events that are irksome rather than the invitation of things that are exciting. So if we start with what bothers us, we have an edge and some leverage for the eventual follow-through required for enacting a change. In this step, it's important to document in our journal all of our Gremlin worries. Anything that sounds like hand-wringing, complaining, and disappointment all gets documented here.

Step 2. Appreciate

It's not all bad news, surely! Knowing what is going well is part of appreciative inquiry. We don't want to throw the baby out with the bathwater. There may be clues as to what needs to be emphasised and strengthened here.

Step 3. Re-orient

I have long espoused that the most powerful and energising question is 'what do I want instead?' Sometimes we have to repeat this question in order to get cut through, as we can get pretty caught up in wailing and moaning about how terrible things are. This is the place to get our focus off what we don't want and steer it to what we do want. When we do this it releases a sense of personal power and autonomy about being the author of our own life once more.

This is also the time to add great detail to our picture of what we do want. We want sensory-rich language across all the senses. One of the practices I use is adapted from my studies of Psych-K. It's about creating a sensory picture of the future you want to create in order to anchor new and supportive beliefs. Psych-K calls it the VAK to the Future.

- *Visual descriptions:* What will you see when things are different? Think in technicolour here.

- *Auditory descriptions:* What will you hear? What will people say? What will you say?
- *Kinaesthetic cues:* What will you feel? Taste? Touch?
- *Emotional:* What emotion comes up when you think of what you want to experience? Where is the most intense part of the feeling in your body when you think of what you want to create? If that feeling had a colour, what would it be? If it had a texture, what would it be? If it had a temperature, what would it be?

Stage two: Upgrade

Step 4. Create a mantra

This is the new belief we want to adopt. Ask: "What do I need to believe about myself in order to experience this new vision?" Generally this starts with an 'I am' For example, you might say, "I am capable and competent."

Step 5. Measure

How will we know if things have changed for better or worse without a gauge? When we have vivid language describing what it is we want to experience, then it is easier to find a measure in it. We need to be able to measure progress. For example, if we described a picture of being able to book travel anywhere in the world in business class, then we have the start of a measure. How much does business class cost to the next favourite destination? Let's say we need $10,000 in a savings account each year to be able to book business class travel. So we can set up a gauge by looking at our savings account and tracking the progress towards the $10,000 mark. We can even make it visible by drawing little thermometer on a post it note with levels on it to show our progress.

Step 6. Meme

This is the story of our future self, told from a present, current perspective. It is so important to journal this. In doing so we will discover the resistance points, the parts that feel unreal, or fraught with resistance, doubt, or low self-worth. Keep writing anyway. If we connect deeply with what we wish to experience, then this will help override internal resistance. The most important part to include in the story of our future self is the 'why'. When we re-connect to our purpose, this helps draw us through our own limiting internal dialogue and Gremlin hand-wringing doubts.

Stage three: Reinforce

Step 7. Rehearse

We want our new belief, our new vision of ourselves to settle in and become our new 'truth' or belief software. We do this through repetition and saturation. In my business mentoring group at Thought Leaders Global, we have a hashtag in our online discussion board that is '#WWABBD' or, 'what would a blackbelt do?' A blackbelt is the top end of income earners, a progression of a business model using the white belt to blackbelt martial arts analogy. A blackbelt is an expert who earns at least $60,000 per month in their practice. By using that meme, the idea is to explore the habits, paradigms, and mental models of someone who has the results we desire. It helps guide attitude, behaviour, and belief, as we adjust to a new reality.

We can do this in other areas of our lives too. I love playing the 'what would an Olympic athlete do in this workout/approach their nutrition/to prioritise sleep?' Or even, 'what would the Dalai Lama do in this situation?' By practising the mindset and behaviours of people we respect and who have the results we wish to emulate, we rehearse for success and become acclimatised to the results.

Step 8. Track

There's a quote, often attributed to Peter Drucker though many others have cited it, "What gets measured gets improved." Sometimes it's not just about improvement, but about taking stock. Keep a lightness about it. Centered leaders are deadly serious about their purpose, but they don't take themselves too seriously. The Dalai Lama is known to be light-hearted. He is serious when he speaks of human rights transgressions, and light-hearted when it comes to treating ourselves a little better.

Recording successes is my favourite way to record progress. I keep a success journal for that very reason. Each day I record either process

Composure

achievements or outcomes. So examples of process achievements would be things like, 'wrote a new article, invited a client to meet about a program, did yoga'. They are activities that lead towards my goals. Outcomes are things that I identified during Step 5 (Measure) that matter to me: number of clients, number of newsletter subscribers, income targets, holidays.

Stacey Barr has a system and program called, PuMP, and a book *Practical Performance Measurement* that takes this to a fine art in an easy-to-follow system. Her premise is to measure what matters and present it in a useful way that shows trends and patterns. In this way we make progress visible at the same time.

Step 9. Anchor

The new belief needs to be anchored in the environment. Repetition and reinforcement with positively charged emotional experiences are critical to creating this new belief software.

I call this part of the process 'pimp the environment'. It means sprucing your surroundings with reminders of the new belief, and why it's important. This helps with acclimatisation to the new mindset, and calms the Gremlin voice.

Some of my favourite strategies for pimping the environment include: daily reminders on my smartphone that pop up with the new belief. I also include positive statements about my goals as if they've been achieved already. Such as, 'My book looks fantastic, I love all the rave reviews!' One strategy when writing this book was the reminder that it was a giant mountain to climb, and one I had been avoiding for years due to tenacious Gremlins. I have since brought this book to the world. The phone reminders have helped me become used to the idea of becoming a published author, and have it be a positive experience in my mind before in reality.

Mark Divine, mentioned previously, calls this a warrior principle of "Win in your mind first." It's a paraphrase from Sun Tzu's *The Art of War.* If you do not feel yourself a winner in your mind before the battle, you will surely lose it.

Other anchoring strategies are vision boards: putting up pictures or words of what we want to experience on a board we see every day.

I use special jewellery that reminds me of what I am creating and intending. I have power dresses that I wear when I am speaking to channel my 'world-class speaker' vision.

Visualisation is a powerful strategy to help anchor the belief and vision. The key to visualisation is to do it with strong and positive feelings. The picture or story needs to come alive in all of our senses in order to be truly effective. This is what helps wire the new belief. Use VAK to the Future in Step 2 as a prompt. Reading that new story to yourself is another way to visualise if you have trouble imagining pictures in the mind's eye.

INSIGHT

From hiking boots to heels

The biggest personal shift I ever made was moving from a 'jeans and fleece' outdoor professional working in not-for-profits to becoming a well-heeled corporate businesswoman and leadership expert.

When I first started my practice in 2002, I knew I had to upgrade many things: wardrobe was one of them. I knew if I wanted to be successful in the business world, I'd need to look the part. I also knew I needed to upgrade my mental software around money. I had worked in the not-for-profit sector for over 20 years, and had held onto very strong beliefs that making money was selfish and materialistic. So I never made any or held on to any for long. My belief software had me rejecting money at emotional, moral, and physical levels.

If I was to be successful in business supporting myself through my expertise and leadership practice, I knew I had to shift these beliefs, or no-one would ever pay me enough for me to support myself! I went to work re-wiring my money belief patterns.

I took myself through the 9-step Belief Buster Matrix:

Stage 1: Review

Step 1 – Diagnose: What was not working? I had no money to do the things I wanted to do such as fly back to Canada to see my family, or save for my future retirement, or even to buy new clothes.

Stage 1: Review

Step 1 – Diagnose: What was not working? I had no money to do the things I wanted to do such as fly back to Canada to see my family, or save for my future retirement, or even to buy new clothes. My money beliefs were having significant impact on my personal as well as professional aspirations to enjoy my life and make a contribution.

Step 2 – Appreciate: What was working, what was right? My desire to be of service in the world was something I held onto. It was then I realised that being of service in the world did not necessarily mean to the exclusion of making money. I did not have to be pauper to be virtuous.

I started to see virtuous and wealthy people around me. This seemed amazing, as it shifted my inner paradigm about what it meant to be wealthy. When Tim Medhurst, the Executive Director of Outward Bound asked me to present to the Fairfax Family Foundation, I was terrified. He wanted me to ask for funds to set up a registered training organisation at Outward Bound, a project near to my heart. These were serious adults from a completely different planet of business – and lots of money.

We asked for $100,000. This was a mind-boggling sum to me at the time. When the cheque arrived, Tim showed it to me and I cried. They gave their own money freely for a cause – one that meant a great deal to me. I was overwhelmed by that generosity. A new light opened for me about my money beliefs: business could be altruistic too. Here were people who could change organisations and change lives through their generosity. A new belief was born in me: the more money you have, the more you have to give. It was a game changer.

Step 3 – Reorient: I wrote a detailed picture of everything I wanted in my life – from partner and home, to clothes and holidays. The list seemed enormous, impossible even! How would I get all that, experience all that, from where I was now? But I stayed true to the process and wrote out the picture, and believed at least in the possibility of it.

Stage 2: Upgrade

Step 4 – Mantra: I had many! Here are a few: "It's safe to have money. It's OK to ask people to pay me for my services. What I have is of value and of service to others. Money is an exchange of energy. I can do good things for myself and others with money."

Step 5 – Measure: I measure my income daily. I have a sheet of paper where I record every cent that comes into my experience. At the end of the month, I add it up and map it against a graph so I can see the trends.

Step 6 – Meme: I kept writing out the story of the various things I wanted to experience. Sometimes the journal writing felt like such a falsehood, and the writing seemed more desperate than faith-filled. Just when I gave up and let go, more money would arrive in the form of new clients or new opportunities.

Stage 3: Reinforce

Step 7 – Rehearse: Over the years, I keep rehearsing the next level up. Now I am playing the 'what would a blackbelt do?' game. It's caused me to make decisions I did not feel ready for, and at the same time reinforced where I am heading, what I am creating. An example of that was investing in my Virtual Assistant.

Just when my practice was becoming more profitable, here was another significant expense. However, I knew that a blackbelt would not be checking their email first thing in the morning, all day and into the evening. Or printing out workbooks, or booking venues. So I took a deep breath and made the investment, trusting that I could generate the income to cover the expense. This was also a good reinforcement of the Abundance mindset I wished to anchor as well – there is always more coming. Hiring my assistant has allowed me to focus on what a blackbelt would do – thinking, writing, creating services and projects that bring value to others.

Step 8 – Track: This has been the most rewarding part. I am now earning several times what I did as an employee, working on amazing international, national, and local leadership projects.

I love seeing my income graph going up, to levels that had previously seemed impossible.

Step 9 – Anchor: I bought myself a custom-designed set of diamond and sapphire earrings. These help anchor my beliefs and new self-image that I am worth it, I can do it, and abundance flows in my life.

It was a confronting process. I had to forgive myself for my past beliefs, and essentially reject who I had been previously. I could no longer be the anti-establishment, 'business people are selfish', altruistic devotee. I had to create new beliefs that money was OK to make and hold. I had to re-imagine what money meant for my world, and the world as a whole.

And so my world changed.

4. Resolve shadow

In the Renewal stage, we balance creation of the new with destruction of the old, like the interaction of Shiva and Shakti. On the hero's journey, Joseph Campbell identifies this process as 'apotheosis', one of the key stages. He explains that it is the expansion of consciousness that the hero experiences after defeating his foe.

In practical terms, apotheosis means facing our own demons. Sometimes, our stories are deep and persistent. When we can own all the aspects of ourselves for which we feel shame, embarrassment, regret or any other lower emotion, then there is potential for apotheosis. This profound sense of expansion of our consciousness lessens personal obstacles towards our objectives.

It means being OK with who we are and who we were.

It means going into the dragon's lair and taming the beast.

Entering the dragon's lair

The journey to the deepest darkest place of the dragon's lair has five distinct phases:

1. Pain. This is the squirmy bit. We can ask ourselves: 'where have I hurt/disappointed/let myself or others down?' Generally we're good at beating ourselves up. We often have extraordinary standards we set for ourselves. If we listen to our own inner conversation we find how unkind and unforgiving of ourselves we can be. By diving into this part of ourselves, it gives us the opportunity to heal and emerge from it stronger. It's much like opening a suppurating wound. Painful and gory, it allows for cleansing and healing.

2. Meaning. This is like rubbing salt in the wound. When we look at past events, it's not often what happened, but what we made it mean: about others, about ourselves, about the world. We can dig right in by asking: 'What am I making this mean? Where did this story come from? Is it true?' Often this involves unleashing a litany of nasty criticism of ourselves and complaints against the world.

3. Release. This is when it starts to get better! Once we purge our systems of our deep painful inner voice, we can sift through the contents. We ask, 'Am I ready to let this go? Am I ready to forgive myself and others?'

Forgiveness is sometimes seen as complex matter. It need not be so. Forgiveness is essentially deciding not to be affected by the stories about the past and to let them go and to choose a new path forward.

Many a future was warped by a grudging attachment to past wrongs. Some of us cling to our old stories like a suit of armour, claiming our victim state in defiance against the world. We can sometimes wear our pain as badge of honour: 'they did this to me – how dare they?' We believe that by reiterating the woes done to us we can somehow become champions of the battle.

In reality, we drag these grudges around like sleds loaded with our bloody armour. We just get slow and tired. Forgiveness is about releasing the story and its hold over us. It's about deciding not to let past wrongs rule the future.

4. Reorient. Once we decide to let go of past stories, we seek something else to light our path. Any shadow has its opposite nearby. We can ask, 'What does the shadow's light side/opposite look feel/sound like?' When we start to look for the light side, we open up to possibilities. This is the art of focusing on what we do want instead of what we don't. Sounds easy, but even this most simple premise can be challenging. If we have not fully let go in the Release stage, we will find our attention drifting to what we don't want.

5. Invite. This is how we start to learn and grow from the depths of our shadow. We ask for support to tame the dragon. Some questions include: 'What do I need to believe? Which archetype can help? How will I keep focus?' Shadow work is ultimately not about slaying the dragon, it's about taming it. There is always the presence of hate where there is love, and always love where there is hate. They are two sides of the same coin. However, we get to choose which side lands up, which side we put to use in the world.

5. Refresh

After facing down our dragons, we'll be in need of some recuperation!

To feel refreshed, we need to undertake daily rituals across the four dimensions of ourselves: physical, mental, emotional, and spiritual. When we focus on the interplay of dimensions, we harness renewal energy.

These are the four daily refresh practices I recommend for leaders:

1. Center

The simplest way to do this is to undertake a 5-15-minute breathing meditation. Deep breathing stimulates the parasympathetic nervous system (the rest and digest systems) while calming the sympathetic (fight or flight) system.

There are a myriad of techniques. Two of my favourites are counting the breath up to ten, and then back down again. If you forget you were meant to be counting, start over.

The other technique is to breathe in for five counts, hold for five counts, release for five counts, hold for 5 counts. This kind of breath control also teaches arousal control. This is a fantastic technique for maintaining emotional control in times of high stress.

2. Appreciate

I use appreciation (generally written in my journal) to help me feel connected to my life, purpose, and the world around me. I practise appreciation rants when I'm driving, and enjoy finding something to appreciate in even the smallest of things.

3. Create

Life is a constant process of creation and experience. By getting deliberate about our focus, we can create experiences by choice, instead of by accident. I use journal exercises to craft new intentions and pictures of the future. When I combine this with visualisation and a mental rehearsal of that possible future, I anchor my intentions and confidence into my subconscious. This way I find myself making choices towards that future more naturally.

4. Purge

Exercise is the number one strategy for any leader to let go of anxiety, mental clutter, and emotional hijacks. It's virtually impossible to worry when labouring in a vigorous workout. The physiological benefits are many; the psychological benefits are profound.

LEADER FOCUS: Andy Vann

Prof, Pom, V-C, and "highly ambitious, somewhat intelligent, and highly flawed human being."

Professor Andrew Vann is a witty and sardonic Englishman who made Australia his home with his young family after training as an engineer and pursuing an academic career. Andy is now the Vice-Chancellor and President of Charles Sturt University based in Bathurst. With campuses around Australia and overseas, Andy has an intensive travel schedule, compounded with multiple professional and personal responsibilities. He knows all too well the absolute necessity of keeping on track with regular refresh practices.

If he puts his self-care routine on the back-burner, his professional engagement suffers. He needs to treat himself as a corporate thoroughbred.

When I first met Andy before he was V-C, he said, "I am running myself ragged and wonder if there might be a better way of doing this leadership thing."

Composure

As his coach, my immediate recommendation was for him to go and lie down under a tree and just 'be' for a while. It was a bit tongue-in-cheek, I admit. My intention however, was completely earnest. He needed to change gears from over-drive into neutral, and quickly. At the time, he was a man who checked his emails while walking from the car to the office, and who did not shut down his computer until well after 11pm on a Sunday. Sitting under a tree, doing *nothing*, was a radical undertaking.

He managed ten minutes. It was a start.

Soon after this conversation, Andy was selected as the Vice-Chancellor of Charles Sturt University. With the increase in responsibility and scope in his new role, Andy knew he had to reform his activity management strategies, or his leadership presence was in danger of short-circuiting.

Andy implemented significant self-management interventions:

He let all his staff know that he would not be looking at emails until at least 24 hours after they had been in his inbox. If it was urgent, they were to contact him by phone. He worked with his Executive Assistant on how to filter, assess, and summarise his emails for batch processing. He blocked out time to deal with the important, but not urgent. He set up regular meetings with his key staff to reduce unscheduled interruptions.

Then he undertook to improve his health management so his energy and renewal tactics kept him in peak condition of the demands of his role. Cycling and running became essentials, even during his busy travel and engagement schedule. He worked on the 'under promise and over deliver' approach to his exercise: something was definitely better than nothing.

For renewal, Andy knew that music and photography were two passions that helped him feel centered. He could then engage more deeply with his spirit and connection with life. He started taking a small ukulele on business trips, and booking in weekend jams at the local Irish pub with musician friends. His photography helped him to focus on the small moments that create a sense of awe, wonder, and delight in life, day-by-day.

Andy, the 'highly flawed human being' is also a balanced and focused one. He knows that his work is a strong passion; he also knows that his family is part of his present and future life too. Rigorous self-care and well-structured renewal practices help him feel even-keeled, fully present in all realms of his world. Of self-management, Andy says, "It's a journey with false starts and ups and downs. I wouldn't want to leave the impression that I can do it perfectly. But I think I can do it well enough to keep myself mostly out of trouble."

Key points for renewal

1. Review
Check your various plans daily, weekly, quarterly, and yearly. Review your 100th birthday and decade themes.

2. Reconnect
This is your chance to connect with trusted advisors, both seen and unseen, and ask for guidance. This includes:

- Advice – from colleagues, coaches, mentors, masterminds, communities of practice
- Interpretation – from guidance cards, therapists, energy workers, or personal review
- Intuition – Check in with your feelings
- Inspiration – prayers, dreams, journaling

3. Reinvent beliefs
Use the nine-step Belief Buster Matrix:

Stage 1: Review
- Step 1 – Diagnose: what's not working?
- Step 2 – Appreciate: what is working?
- Step 3 – Re-orient: what do I want instead?

Stage 2: Upgrade
- Step 4 – Mantra: "I am…"
- Step 5 – Measure: Evidence to be gathered
- Step 6 – Meme: story of the future I am creating.

Stage 3: Reinforce
- Step 7 – Rehearse: practice new belief and anticipated reality
- Step 8 – Track: measure progress
- Step 9 – Anchor: physical reminder of what I am creating.

4. Resolve shadow

This is about entering the Dragon's Lair and facing your shadow side:

- Pain – where have I hurt/disappointed/let myself or others down?
- Release – am I ready to let this go?
- Meaning – what did I make this mean?
- Re-orient – what do I want instead?
- Invite – invite support and new perspective.

5. Refresh

These are the four daily refresh practices:

- Center – breathing practice
- Appreciate – journal and appreciation rants
- Create – visualise, write the future
- Purge – exercise.

The Path Of Totality

Oneness is the sense of deep connection to all things: human, animal, elemental. Leaders who lead from Oneness do it not from a sense of selflessness, but from a sense of totality. It is a deep sense of stewardship that they bring to every conversation, every deed, every decision.

Oneness University says, 'we are not independent, but interdependent.' Some describe the sense of interconnection as being like waves on an ocean. Unique with our perspective, yet part of the whole. So we are alone, together.

We have our unique perspective, our unique view of the world, our own private experiences, and yet they are universal too. We cry when we see the pain of others, we smile when we see joy in others. We expand and feel better for it. Oneness is the deepest of all compassion: what affects you, affects me, and I want to help if I can – for your benefit, for my benefit, for all our benefit.

Choosing Oneness as the path for centered leadership

Living in fear, and from an alone perspective, we experience a shrinking, a shying away from life, an avoidance of risk, of change, of growth. It is a state of contraction that serves nothing and no-one. It is however the staging ground for enormous growth once we realise we are trapped in a place of diminishment.

Living in fear as a group outlook breeds all sorts of limiting and problematic world views. This is tribalism, factionalism, 'us versus them', good versus evil, black versus white. It shakes the world into lower vibrations of conflict, defensiveness/aggressiveness, and extremism. The only good news is the recognition that there is power in togetherness, even if it is from an isolationist point of view.

Living in faith, alone, allows a new dimension. A sliver of hope and the resonance of love into our experience. When we move into this space, we can feel the embrace of peace in our world, even when the world is not peaceful. From here we can spread calm through our own presence, and like the warm light of campfire in the darkness, we draw others to us.

Living in faith from a collective perspective places us in the realm of centered leadership. We become public and articulate about our purpose and concern for our fellow human beings. We care for those in front of us, and those we have not met. We make decisions that uplift others, that inspire others, that support the planet and humanity as a whole. It filters our reactions into composite and caring responses. We become a wise and healing presence, able to respond with wisdom and compassion.

We become ready to shift the universe.

INSIGHT

Learning to live in faith

When I was diagnosed with cancer, I worked out I had choice: live in fear, or live in faith.

Statistics and probabilities aside, the outcome was uncertain. I decided that my best chance of survival, or of at least enduring the treatment, was to make choices based on a positive focus.

This was not easy by any means. Cancer treatment is invasive.

Being positive was to turn away from the horror that filled me as my body swam with toxic chemicals.

Faith was a wisp of light in a fog of chemo nausea. I clung to it.

Having been raised without religion, this wasn't religious faith. It became a spiritual experience. Trying to find meaning when confronted with a potentially lethal disease at the age of 35 raised all sorts of metaphysical issues for me.

Mind-body connection was one of them. "Is there anything I can do to aid my healing?" I asked my surgeon. He said, "There is nothing you can do to fix this." Talk about disempowering! Not one to take such a directive or dismissal of my own autonomous powers and determination, I set out to look after myself anyway.

I saw a nutritionist, I had massages, I sought the help of hands-on alternative therapies. I had trouble believing any of it – it sounded all so woo-woo.

Slowly I allowed myself to contemplate the 'what if it's true?' question. 'What if it's true I can change my biology with my focus? What if it's true that thoughts affect things? What if it's true I will live?' These all felt much better than wondering, 'What if I can't have kids? What if the cancer comes back? What if I die?' I took my first fledgling step towards my version of living in faith.

I started to see the world with new eyes. Small things became huge miracles: how a bulb becomes a plant and produces the most exquisite flower; how ants build complex systems; the play of golden light on the grass in the winter afternoon as I made my daily few steps outside, clutching my wounded tummy.

I started to feel a deep connection and love for my surroundings. I remembered other moments of wonder. A star-still winter night in Winnipeg, the air harsh as needles, gazing in awe at the endless stars. The moonlight soaking a quiet silver lake late one night with a friend as we sat up and shared our young girls' dreams on a canoeing adventure. I felt held in the palm of the universe again.

The poem *Desiderata*, by Max Ehrmann, filled my heart:

"You are a child of the universe, no less than the trees and the stars; you have a right to be here. And whether or not it is clear to you, no doubt the universe is unfolding as it should."

So began my discovery and unfolding sense of Oneness.

LEADER FOCUS: Dr David Cooke

How Konica Minolta's Managing Director ingrains daily social responsibility into a global organisation.

I met Dr David Cooke at a public speaking program. He seemed quiet yet open to the experience, to the situation, to me. He kept to himself during the classroom presentations but was happy to chat in the breaks. He seemed relaxed, grounded, and gentle. And something else.

When Matt Church the presenter came over to us during one of the exercises and spoke to him with obvious deference and respect, I was intrigued. Who was this quiet, humble man sitting with me? Matt waxed lyrical about David's culture change initiatives at Konica Minolta and his corporate social responsibility ethos.

David had written a PhD on the mutual, synergistic benefits of corporate social responsibility (CSR) and engagement with not-for-profits. As the first non-Japanese Managing Director of Konica Minolta Australia, David had famously raised his hand to ask a question of the President of Konica Minolta. In a Japanese company, to challenge the President publicly was not done. David's question centered on what the company was doing for and in the community. The President answered that donating profits to charities made employees more interested and engaged in their work. The work felt more purposeful.

This resonated with David. He wanted to work with an organisation that valued global citizenship and stewardship as much as he did. As MD in Australia, David developed Konica Minolta's corporate social responsibility as an ingrained aspect of day-to-day business. This principle and approach has also been adapted globally as a key tenet of the organisation. Being a company that cares is core to its business. It now supports various charities globally and locally as part of its key business practice.

In Australia, David invited the staff to nominate which charities to support in the health, education, and environment sectors.

They chose Landcare Australia, Breast Cancer Network Australia, and The Smith Family. David added a fourth (where he is a board member), Project Futures, to help end human trafficking.

In an interview, David explains one of the key benefits of having CSR programs. Staff are invited to volunteer at the nominated charities. He says you can tell the ones who have previously volunteered: "They're the ones whose eyes light up." David has a strong conviction that business is about both making money *and* contributing to the wellbeing of a society.

Before he had a reputation and status as MD, David had commitment. He has a long-standing transcendental meditation practice, for which he has been called a "hippy in a suit."[7] Matt Church has also called him a "cross between Genghis Khan and Gandhi'", reflecting the corporate and more reflective sides. David connects daily with source energy, stills his mind, and resonates deeply with all that is. This is how he cultivates the essence of compassion to channel it into his corporate activities.

So how does David show up as a leader? He is quiet, and yet open. When I had a meeting with one of his staff about a leadership development program, I dropped in to say a brief hello, not wanting to disturb him. Whatever he was doing, he stopped and invited me in for a conversation. During the ten minutes he spent with me, he was fully present, engaged, calm, and friendly. His eyes danced with good humour and genuine interest. There was no sign of any pressing issue lurking behind him, blinking on the computer screen, though I knew, as he told me, he was in the middle of negotiating a deal worth several millions of dollars. And yet I was all that mattered in that moment.

I felt honoured. The MD of one of Australia's big companies stopped his calendar to connect with a fellow human being.

Connection first, task later.

I am sure this is how David wins the hearts and minds of his staff. There is an acknowledgment of corporate goals and

---

7   Renegade Collective, Issue 17: http://shop.collectivehub.com/collections/
    magazine/products/issue-seventeen

services, and there is also a cultural imperative that people are foremost in the picture. His global consciousness channels his focus and shapes his approach to his leadership role. He blends this polarity: a focus on the staff, for their own sake, and a focus on others, for the planet.

David is a true global steward who can still be completely engaged in the present moment with the people around him. Each person matters. The issues are global, the awareness extended, and yet his connection is immediate and present.

David's ever-present sense of Oneness frames his corporate purpose. He sees the corporate agenda as just one of many avenues to pursue custodianship of Oneness and uplifting of humanity. He chose the boardroom over a beach retreat. Though he does not eliminate that option by any means from his future!

Our responsibility as centered leaders

We are responsible not only for ourselves, but for how we bring our presence to create good in and for the world.

As Vice-Chancellor, leader Andy Vann feels deeply the stewardship his role entails. His self-management is key to ensuring he can deliver on his purpose and vision of the university. He advocates for the central and essential role of universities in local communities, and has deepened this option by adopting with permission an aphorism from the Wiradjuri, *yindyamarra winhanga-nha*, which translates as 'the wisdom of respectfully knowing how to live well in a world worth living in'. It resonates with his strong promotion of Charles Sturt University as an institution with 'soul'. He writes:

"Soul power. With apologies to James Brown, I wanted to start by talking about the notion of 'soul' for an organisation. This was one of the concepts that was in my mind at the start of the year as it struck me that CSU really seemed to have it. My working definition of this would be an organisation that sees you, recognises you and responds to you. I think we will all have had the experience of engaging with organisations who seem the very opposite. My sense is that by and large we do a pretty good job of this at CSU, although I would

also be sure that at least some people will have different stories to tell. However, for a university I think we should be aiming to sustain a strong sense of community and to be seen to have a soul."[8]

Andy brings the concept of soul alive in an institution. He filters his plans and decisions through the lens of service to community and what he believes higher education ought to be about.

Leaders like Andy Vann and David Cooke show us what we need on small and large scales: intimate engagement with every human soul as well as stewardship for community and planet.

Our responsibilities as centered leaders then include conversations with the very words of love, compassion, and soul in business life. This is what our hearts and minds long for. We want and need organisations that speak to the core of who we are. We need centered leaders to call attention to purpose beyond shuffling papers.

---

8 http://blog.csu.edu.au/2012/08/09/further-thoughts-on-strategy-mission-and-narrative/

Key points for Oneness

- See self as part of the whole – a branch on the tree, a wave on the ocean
- Base decisions on what is best for the elevated whole, long-term
- Help bring the sense of purpose and Oneness to the world of work by talking about vision, contribution, love and soul in the workplace
- Be brave
- Have faith.

A Call To Action: Elevate Consciousness

We know when they arrive. They have a certain energy, a vibe, a kind of magnetic pull. People hush and want to listen when they speak. What makes a Nelson Mandela, a Barack Obama, a Mother Theresa, a Dr Kiran Bedi, a Kofi Annan so compelling? Is it charisma? Is it power? Is it command?

Composed leaders with distinctive presence:

- Don't hurry, they are deliberate and focused
- Don't intimidate, they uplift and inspire
- Are serious but enjoy a joke
- Are humble and step up to be responsible
- Are patient and decisive when required, and
- No-one is beneath their respect and attention.

It boils down to our BE – THINK – DO.

How to BE

We have a deep awareness of our own vulnerability, of our own open heart that is deeply authentic and transparent. Strong vulnerability does not mean weak. It means accepting all of one's self, one's strengths and challenges, and not hiding from owning one's mistakes and failing.

We have a deep connection to our personal values. They govern all our choices and focus.

We have a larger-than-ourselves sense of purpose. Our life's work is about contribution and meaning.

We speak from a place of Oneness and of the deep abiding awareness that we, and all things, are interconnected and interdependent.

How to THINK

We think in systems, paradox, and polarities. Nothing is black and white nor linear.

We can consider the individual and the collective at the same time.

We communicate in metaphors, parables, and models.

We consider the context and impact on multiple generations, multiple communities, multiple nations.

We look for the win-win-win solutions.

How to DO

We have world-class self-mastery habits.

We have a regular self-reflective practice that may also be spiritual.

We seek guidance from both internal and external worlds, from both practical and mystical sources.

We are fastidious with who and what we surround ourselves with to allow the best thinking and inspiration.

We coach other leaders to be, think, and do more.

We are extraordinary communicators. We can distil the essence of our message succinctly and use a palette of expressions and language that reaches all audiences.

Charisma helps. Charm and friendliness are very compelling, but they're not the whole story. We need depth as well as sparkle. In fact, strength of spirit and character will make the difference between a charismatic flash in the pan and a shining beacon.

Physicality matters. Being tall and good-looking is an added bonus, not a requirement. Standing tall, shoulders back with confidence and openness will make up for much lack of stature. Voice modulation, accent, gestures – these are all important aspects of presence, but they are the bow that gets the box noticed. Content and value trump wrapping and fluff.

A call to action: elevate consciousness

The world needs centered leaders.

If we had leaders who focused their quest in service to others and to the planet, we would have less selfishness and more contribution.

If we had leaders who chose to enact their quest by living into better version of themselves, we would have less jealousy and more humility.

If we had a world where leaders spoke the truth, with love, compassion, and wisdom, then words of anger would fade.

If we had a world with leaders who felt their feelings fully, and allowed them to ebb and flow without necessarily acting on them, we would have a more humane civilisation.

If we had leaders who found the space to respond with love rather than react in anger, we would have less violence.

If we had world full of leaders who strove to learn, to grow, to contribute, then we would have collaborative engagement and accelerated breakthroughs for common challenges like climate change, food security, access to clean water and improved health.

If we had leaders who pause to reflect, to recharge, to reconnect with spirit, we would find our societies evolving peacefully.

We don't have a world of centered leaders without leaders choosing this path, one by one. This is the call to the quest, for life of growth through adventure and service.

Will you be one of us?

Citations

Introduction

Beck, D. and Gowan, C., 2005. *Spiral Dynamics: Mastering values, leadership, and change.* Malden: Blackwell; Reprint edition

The Elders: http://theelders.org/

Wigglesworth, C., 2014. *SQ 21: The Twenty-One Skills of Spiritual Intelligence,* New York: Select Books

Bedi, K., 2010 – *It's Always Possible: Transforming One Of The Largest Prisons In The World.* New Delhi: Sterling Publishers Private Limited; Eighth reprint edition

Chapter 1 – Growth

Secretan, L., 2010. *The Spark, The Flame, and the Torch: Inspire Self. Inspire Others. Inspire the World.* Caledon: The Secretan Center Inc.

Sinek, S., 2011. *Start With Why: How Great Leaders Inspire Everyone To Take Action.* New York: Portfolio

Simon Sinek's 2009 TEDx Talk: '*How Great Leaders Inspire Action*': http://www.ted.com/talks/simon_sinek_how_great_leaders_inspire_action?language=en

Campbell, J., 2008. *The Hero with a Thousand Faces (The Collected Works of Joseph Campbell).* 3rd edition. Novato: New World Library

Divine, M., 2014. *Unbeatable Mind: Forge Resiliency and Mental Toughness To Succeed at an Elite Level.* 3rd edition. Kindle edition: Mark Divine

Chapter 2 – Focus

Pearson, C., 1991. *Awakening the Heroes Within: Twelve Archetypes to Help Us Find Ourselves and Transform Our World.* 1st edition. New York: HarperCollins

Campbell, J. 2008. ———

Divine, M., 2014. ———

Chapter 3 – Contribution

Godin, S., 2008. *Tribes: We Need You To Lead Us.* 1st edition. London: Portfolio

Wilber, K., 2011. *The Essential Ken Wilber: An Introductory Reader.* Kindle edition. Boston: Shambhala

Cialdini, R., 2009. *Influence: The Psychology of Persuasion.* Kindle edition. Sydney: HarperCollins e-books

Amy Cuddy TED Global Talk 2012: *Your Body Language Shapes Who You Are:* http://www.ted.com/talks/amy_cuddy_your_body_language_shapes_who_you_are?language=en

Chapter 4 – Connection

Aikido: http://www.aikidoaus.com.au

Church, M. 2002. *High Life 24/7: Balance Your Body Chemistry and Feel Uplifted.* Seaforth: Thought Leaders Limited; 2007 reprint edition

Goleman D., 2006. *Social Intelligence: The New Science of Human Relationships.* New York: Hutchinson., pp 68-72

Chapter 5 – Renewal

Einstein, A., 2006. *The World As I See It.* USA: Stellar Essentials © 2014

Osho, 1994. *Osho Zen Tarot The Transcendental Game of Zen Cards.* Dublin: Boxtree Limited, second edition

Ryde, R., 2007. *Thought Leadership: Moving Hearts and Minds.* 1st edition. London: Palgrave Macmillan

Beck, M. 2008. *Steering by Starlight: The Science and Magic of Finding Your Destiny.* New York: Rodale Books

Chopra, D., 2005. *Synchrodestiny: Harnessing the Infinite Power of Coincidence to Create Miracles.* Reading: Rider

Psych-K: https://www.psych-k.com/

Barr, S., 2014. *Practical Performance Measurement: Using the PuMP Blueprint for Fast, Easy and Engaging KPIs.* Samford: The PuMP Press.

Divine, M., 2014. ———

Sun Tzu, 2007. *The Art of War.* Minneapolis Filiquarian

Chapter 6 – Oneness

Oneness University: http://onenessuniversity.org/

Ehrmann, M. 1995. *Desiderata: A Poem For A Way of Life.* New York: Crown

Acknowledgements

A special thank you to Matt Church and Peter Cook of Thought Leaders Global for your encouragement and faith. I also wanted to acknowledge the community of conscious leaders you have created that are shifting engagement with others in such a strong positive way. Thank you also to my Thought Leaders mentor Rod Buchecker, who has been there in the high times and supported me when I dipped through some tougher times. I continue to be uplifted and inspired by the company I keep in Thought Leaders Business School.

Thank you to my assistant Lisa Wilmott who keeps the machinery of business ticking over smoothly, and to Rebecca Stewart, my editor for her sound advice and support of the book.

To the astounding leaders I have had the pleasure to spend time with, thank you for letting me share your story: Dr David Cooke, Professor Andy Vann, Colin Hendrie, and Bianca Jurd. For Dr Kiran Bedi, thank you for being a lighthouse for truth and compassion, worldwide.

To my all clients, past and present, I have learned so much from each of you! It is privilege to assist you on your Hero's Journey.

To my personal advisor, Jason Irving, thank you for your ongoing assistance on my spiritual journey and for helping me find a way through cancer into a life of health and freedom.

For my family who love me even when I'm 'hangry' and have cranky pants, thank you for putting up with me. You keep me humble and human.

For Rob, who reminds me regularly that life is for living. With you, every day is a day to be happy.

About The Author

Leadership expert Zoë Routh inspires leaders and their teams to thrive. As a speaker and mentor, she challenges established leadership thinking and helps build stronger business culture through courage, wisdom and compassion.

Originally Canadian, Zoë's career began in Northwest Ontario, leading canoe trips through the rugged Canadian wilderness. In 1996 she moved to Australia to work with Outward Bound, where she developed nationally recognised outdoor leadership training programs.

Now a naturalized Aussie, Zoë has made her mark around the country. As Program Manager at the Australian Rural Leadership Foundation, she developed national change and leadership programs for groups as diverse as the Telstra Foundation and the Wine Industry Future Leaders Program. She also speaks regularly on issues facing industry leadership today.

Zoë works closely with senior leaders in higher education, SES level public service, and the private sector.

Her thirst for outdoor adventure regularly takes her around the country. She enjoys telemark skiing, has run six marathons, and loves hiking in the high country. She is married to a gorgeous Aussie and is mother to six garden-wrecking chooks.

Read more about Zoë's work at www.innercompass.com.au